Diplomacy for the Next Century

Abba Eban

Diplomacy for the
Next Century

Yale University Press   New Haven & London

Designed by Rebecca Gibb. Set in Bembo and Meta types by Keystone Typesetting, Inc. Printed in the United States of America by Vail-Ballou Press, Binghamton, New York.

Library of Congress Cataloging-in-Publication Data
Eban, Abba Solomon, 1915–
      Diplomacy for the next century / Abba Eban.
         p.   cm.
      Includes bibliographical references and index.
      ISBN 0-300-07287-2 (cloth : alk. paper)
      1. Diplomacy.   2. International relations.   3. Israel—Foreign relations administration.   I. Title.
   JZ1305.E22   1998
   327—dc21   97-39250
                                                                    CIP

A catalogue record for this book is available from the British Library.

10 9 8 7 6 5 4 3

This book began as the Castle Lectures in Yale's Program in Ethics, Politics, and Economics, delivered by Abba Eban at Yale University in 1993 and 1994.

The Castle Lectures were endowed by Mr. John K. Castle. They honor his ancestor, the Reverend James Pierpont, one of Yale's original founders. Given by established public figures, Castle Lectures are intended to promote reflection on the moral foundations of society and government, and to enhance understanding of ethical issues facing individuals in our complex modern society.

Contents

A Credentials Ceremony: September 15, 1950

It occurred to me that I was sitting a few yards away from the most powerful leader in the history of mankind. More powerful than the Babylonian and Persian emperors, than Alexander the Great, Julius Caesar, Napoleon, the rulers of the British Empire at its zenith, or the Russian and German dictators of the twentieth century.

There never has been a time when one nation held such predominant military and economic power as that of the United States after World War II. America had attained this primacy during a conflict in which all the other participants had suffered defeat, or devastation, or exhaustion, or all of them together. The United States had a monopoly of nuclear weapons, created 50 percent of the world's product, and dominated the voting systems in the newly established international agencies.

As I looked at President Truman, I wondered if power had ever been expressed with such total absence of pomp or pretension. He was about five feet nine inches tall, with square shoulders, a long sharply edged nose, steel-rimmed spectacles, and grey-white hair cut with care and precision and smoothly brushed.

The White House was undergoing repairs, and neighboring Blair House, in which Truman would pass nearly all seven years of his presidency, was a substantial middle-class home, less majestic than some tens of thousands of homes across the land. The air conditioner was more well meaning than effective, and the presidential countenance was bathed in perspiration. Truman's jacket was missing, and his plain white shirt was framed by suspenders of a glaring red hue. If you passed him in the street of a small town, you would imagine that he was on the way to an office in a central part of a moderately sized building. If there was such a thing as an "imperial presidency," nobody had broken the news to Harry S. Truman of Independence, Missouri.

The occasion of our encounter was the presentation of my credentials as Ambassador of Israel to the United States. Obedient to the chief of protocol who accompanied me on this mission, I had dressed in formal clothing with the conventional silver-grey tie and bore with me the bulky documents wrapped in leather containing the letters of credence which would assure President Truman that I really was what I purported to be, namely, the Ambassador Extraordinary and Envoy Plenipotentiary of the State of Israel to the United States of America. I was thirty-four years old and understandably nervous.

Credentials are formulated almost entirely in capital letters, and are rarely noted for literary grace or innovation. It was evident that the President feared I might follow tradition and actually declaim the text. In order to preempt this peril, he moved with vigor and precision. He snatched the document from my hands and said: "Let's cut out the crap and have a real talk!" He then cast a triumphant glare at the disconcerted chief of protocol who had rehearsed me for a far more elegant ritual. It was soon to emerge that Truman regarded his own State Department as a hostile foreign power.

This was not the first time I had encountered President Truman's apathy about protocol. In May 1948 President Chaim

Weizmann paid a first state visit to Washington. It was naturally considered appropriate for an Israeli gift to be presented at the White House. The choice fell, understandably, on a Torah scroll. The trouble was that nobody in our embassy had troubled to explain what this article was. The gift was duly introduced into the presidential presence by a member of Truman's staff. It was clear from the confused look on the President's face that he had no idea for what purpose this unfamiliar article could be applied. He looked with unassuaged curiosity at the blue velvet cover, the golden thread, and the jangling bells. Meanwhile, one of his senior White House staff, probably Clark Clifford, could be heard whispering that it was incumbent on the President to say a word of thanks. Truman rose nobly to the occasion. Directing a broad smile to President Weizmann, he uttered immortal words: "Thank you very much, Mr. President, I've always wanted one of these."

Truman's first question to me that September was a deferential inquiry about President Weizmann's health. This illustrated his tendency to see international politics in strictly human terms. Truman had been captivated by Weizmann's dignity and tact, whereas he was totally alienated from the official Zionist leadership. This caused us delicate problems, for real power in Zionism lay no longer with the deposed elder statesman but with Abba Hillel Silver, the reigning chief of American Zionism, and David Ben-Gurion, who was the undoubted leader of Palestinian Jewry. But Truman held Silver in severe aversion, regarding him, not inaccurately, as a supporter of the Republican party, which came second only to the Soviet Union as a primary target of his distrust. Truman was strangely indifferent to Ben-Gurion's qualities and met him only once during his presidency. It was useless to tell him that there were new leaders in Zionism. Truman seemed to believe that if you were President of the United States you could decide with whom you would or would not hold discourse.

Once, in March 1948, when there was a crucial need to prevent a defection from American support of Jewish statehood, and when only direct access to the President could achieve this aim, the Zionists had to bring Weizmann in querulous mood some thousands of miles across the ocean.

Even then it was not easy to secure an interview, for Truman was firm in his resolve to refuse contact with any Zionist leader whatsoever, suspecting them all of "emotionalism." In a handwritten note to a White House aide he had included Arabs and Latin Americans in this accusation, adding a prayer to God that "the children of Israel would get an Isaiah and the Christians a St. Paul, while the Arabs would get some insight into the Sermon on the Mount."

It was possible to get Weizmann into Blair House on that occasion only by allowing Truman's former business partner, Eddie Jacobson, to persuade him that Weizmann corresponded in Jewish history to the southern President, Andrew Jackson, whose sculptured portrait adorned Truman's office. My own view as a student of history is and was that no two human beings who ever walked on earth had fewer common attributes than Andrew Jackson and Chaim Weizmann, but since the establishment of a Jewish state was of higher interest for me than historical accuracy, I was prepared to join the preposterous Jackson-Weizmann analogy for the forty-eight hours necessary for the crucial visit to take place. I told Jacobson that if anyone met Weizmann and Andrew Jackson together, he would find it hard to tell them apart.

In the brief credentials ceremony, Truman's sentences flowed without any expectation that his voice or formulations would rise even spasmodically above the solid, flat farming earth in which he had been nurtured. Yet there was no difficulty in grasping the core of his thought. He said twice that the decision to drop the atomic bomb on Hiroshima had caused him no anguish or discomfort. From this irrelevance I deduced that his anguish and discomfort must have been intense. He warned me again to beware of the striped-pants boys in the State Department, staring reproachfully at the unstriped pants of the chief of protocol.

I deduced from this experience that Truman's greatest gift lay not in expression but in decision. In this his courage and independence were exemplary. He did not hedge or support opposing contingencies so as to claim rectitude after any result. The abundance of his influential decisions is extraordinary. He decided to devastate Hiroshima and Nagasaki with nuclear weapons, to force Soviet troops out of Iran, to assume the responsibilities which Britain abandoned in Turkey and Greece, to offer Marshall Plan aid to Western and Eastern Europe, to accept Eastern Europe's rejection of it with serenity, to establish the North Atlantic Treaty Organization in order to contain Soviet expansion, to resist the North Korean invasion of South Korea, to dismiss Gen. Douglas MacArthur for insubordination, to despise Sen. Joseph McCarthy in strident terms, to recognize Israel, thus fixing the parameters of the postwar Middle East, and, finally, to fight a successful election campaign which he seemed to have no chance of winning.

Most of these decisions can be applauded or criticized, but it is hard to withhold respect for Truman's unprecedentedly assertive use of the presidential power and for his unexpected success in securing an atmosphere of consensus in its behalf.

Truman's decisions were epoch-making in every sense of the term, but they fell from him with no accompanying show of emotion. He gave the impression of ticking them off on a yellow pad in a drily level mood. He was greatly admired during the Cold War years. In the aftermath of the Vietnam debacle and during the détente period, his presidency became the subject of revisionist criticism. He was judged to have shown a greater talent for resistance than for initiative. The test came when containment had secured its objective and the adversary might have been ready for accommodation. Some believe that this moment was already reached in 1949, when the Soviet Union was sufficiently impressed by American power to be ready for compromise. Truman and his advisers, especially the severe secretary of state, Dean Acheson, never pursued the possibility of a transition from confrontation to negotiation, and the Cold War was passed on to the successor generation with its temperature unchanged.

The harmony between President and secretary of state was remarkable when we reflect on their disparate temperaments and their divergent habits of speech, dress, and idiom. Acheson, who shares with Truman the credit for bold decisionmaking, was a man with many certainties and few doubts. He regarded public opinion and the Congress as intruders who sometimes had to be humored and placated more out of constitutional loyalty than through any real hope that they would add enlightenment.

By the end of the Truman administration the picture of the postwar era was clearly drawn. Red lines against encroachment were fixed in Europe and Washington had become the center of the free world's military, political, and economic struggle against communism. Militarily, the United States' commanding nuclear arsenal and its unchallenged air and naval power protected its allies against Communist aggression. Economically, it had revived the war-ravaged nations of Western Europe and had created the institutional structures—the International Monetary Fund, the World Bank, and the General Agreement on Tariffs and Trade—for the postwar international economic system. Politically, the United States had seen its dream of the United Nations realized and had discharged a moral obligation to the survivors of the Holocaust by helping the establishment and consolidation of the State of Israel.

With all his knowledge of the world and his own place in its future, Truman was utterly immune to the intoxications of summitry and unimpressed by ceremonies. He made few voyages outside the country during his presidency. Until his journey to Potsdam in 1945 he had never left the continental United States except while serving in the American Army in World War I.

Arriving in Berlin in 1945, in sobriety of spirit and modesty of expectation, he wrote to his wife: "I can't get Chanel No. 5 . . . there is none to be had—not even on the black market . . . or in Paris. But I managed to get some other kind for $6.00 at the American P. X. They said it is equal to No. 5 and sells for $35.00 an ounce at home. So if you don't like it, a profit can be made on it. . . . I seem to have Joe and Winnie [Stalin and Churchill] talking to themselves and both are exceedingly careful with me. Uncle Joe gave his dinner last night. There were at least 25 toasts—so much getting up and sitting down that there was practically no time to eat or drink either—a very good thing. Being the super duper guest I pulled out at 11 o'clock after a lovely concert."

After presenting my credentials on that September morning in 1950, I waited for the next ambassador to emerge from his presidential encounter. This was Hermann Van Roijen of the Netherlands. I asked him what the President had said to him. He replied: "He told me for some reason that he had never lost any sleep over the decision to drop atomic bombs on Japan."

For all his dedication to international causes, Truman was essentially a parochial American living close to his original soil and faintly suspicious of the external domain. He was capable of conventional vulgarities in referring to foreigners in unflattering terms. World War II broke down his provincialism and equipped him to speak and act for an America that had renounced the dream of a fortress existence and moved with the impulse of the modern age.

Seven years after the shock of becoming President, the architect of great decisions slipped away from Eisenhower's unmemorable inauguration speech, made his way to the railroad station, and chugged back to Independence, Missouri, without any Secret Service accompaniment. He didn't feel that anything was very different. He gathered his friends around him and played cards as he used to do in the past—probably with the same friends.

Nothing much had happened to him, except that he had changed the world.

1 The Cold War Remembered

Few people in 1989 were predicting that the Cold War was about to end. Conventional "wisdom" told us that the East-West tension in Europe would dominate the international system for several more decades. The idea that the Communist empire would perish without a blood-bath was regarded as fantasy. Slogans about a "roll-back" of Soviet power and the "liberation" of the Eastern European satellite regimes had been heard at various times during the Cold War, but they had carried no conviction.

Meanwhile, there was a fatalistic acceptance of "the balance of terror" in which thousands of nuclear warheads were directed at crowded cities in America and the Soviet Union. The most optimistic view was that the Western powers and the Soviet bloc would maintain their confrontation—but without an explosion of nuclear madness.

No wonder the collapse of Communist rule in Eastern Europe took the world by surprise. Sovietology was the humiliated science. Despite the proliferation of university chairs, institutes, brain trusts, seminars, colloquiums, and a bibliography of oceanic proportions, not a single authoritative voice had predicted the early demise of Soviet power. Apart from a deterministic conviction that all empires are ultimately mortal, mankind seemed content with the bleak stabilities of the Cold War. It was a world in which antagonisms and fidelities were clearly defined. The Cold War was agreeable neither as a reality nor as a prospect, but we all knew exactly where we stood.

The end of Communist power, symbolized by the crumbling of the Berlin Wall, the vengeful destruction of Lenin's statues, and the emergence of free-market societies in the Soviet Union, was primarily the result of impulses at work within the Soviet system itself. The Soviet empire was grotesquely overextended. The chaotic pluralism of its nationalities, the rusty obsolescence of its technologies, disguised by selective triumphs in a few publicized fields, the decadence of its economy, and the grotesque brutalities of its suppressions came together in an incoherent medley of symptoms, all pointing to instability. But when the collapse occurred, the salient question was not why the Communist empire had disintegrated, but why and how it had lasted so long.

Yet for many years the Soviet Union had looked and sounded like a success story. From being an outlaw state on the margin of the international system, threatened by a powerful Germany to the west and a dynamic Japan to the east, regarded as chronically backward in science and productivity, huddled up against hostile neighbors in Central European and Baltic states, the Soviet Union had attained the status of a world power comparable to the United States and overshadowing all others. All the contiguous states in Europe except Finland were under Russian control. Russia's dominance in East Germany and Czechoslovakia had pushed its imperial control further west than the czars had ever dared to penetrate. In the specific proportions of Russian history, the Soviet Union stood tall and proud. It had recuperated all the losses of the Russo-Japanese war and World War I. It had reached the highest pinnacle of power that any Russian regime had ever been able to celebrate.

The Soviet Union could also take satisfaction from a feeling of psychological revenge. Russian emissaries used to be received at European courts and chanceries with a supercilious courtesy as representatives of a lower social and political culture seeking to be patronized by European elites. After World War II Soviet leaders aroused apprehensive deference, without ever seeking affection. Yet despite Soviet diplomatic and military successes, the great Soviet colossus suddenly crumbled and joined the ranks of defunct empires.

With astonishing speed, a revisionist theme about the Cold War has infected the consciousness of the West. It proclaims that the Soviet threat was never real, that the fears of Europeans and Americans were mere hypochondria, that America and its allies deserve no credit for a Soviet collapse that would have happened in any case. An article in *Time* magazine in January 1990 brings all these illusions together in small space. In Henry Kissinger's words, *Time* asserted that "America had not really won the cold war but that the Soviet Union had lost it, and four decades of effort had therefore been unnecessary because things would have worked out equally well—or perhaps better—had America left them alone."[1]

Articles like the one in *Time* magazine should not be lightly tossed aside; they should be thrown energetically into the fire. The deterministic theory of communism's self-destruction cannot be sustained. If the United States had not faced the Soviet Union with a great concentration of deterrent power and an alternative ideology of freedom, the Cold War could have led to a Communist triumph in Europe, which America would have been compelled ultimately to resist. That American tenacity with European endorsement preserved the freedoms of the world is beyond reasonable doubt.

There is room for the hypothesis that the possibility of modifying Cold War tensions by a more perceptive Western approach should have been examined at earlier stages, notably when Joseph Stalin died in 1953. It is also true that for many years the Western powers lived under the delusion that the Communist world was a monolith, united under the slogan "international communism." Diversity of interests and attitudes within the Communist system could have been diagnosed earlier and this might have opened possibilities for a more imaginative diplomacy. This, however, is mere speculation. The theme of Western policy was deterrence, which is the science of things that do not occur. Historians have a tendency to imagine the past and to describe the future. There is no way of knowing with certainty whether courses not taken would have had specific and tangible effects. The Cold War ended in victory with the Communist empire in collapse, and victory, unlike defeat, is a matter for celebration, not for laborious inquests.

The gravest danger had emerged immediately after World War II, when possible Communist take-overs in France and Italy had threatened European democracy. The ease with which Czechoslovakia was communized in 1948 illustrated how near the West was to its own eclipse. To hail the victory of the West does not require us to validate every phase of the Western anti-Communist strategy. The most important thing about a war is how it ends and who wins.

There were five years during which it seemed likely that the Cold War would burst into flame. This was between 1948 and 1953. The Soviet Union tried and failed to blockade West Berlin and was frustrated by Truman's airlift. The United States orchestrated the establishment of the North Atlantic Treaty Organization (1949). The Soviets exploded their first nuclear warhead, thus terminating the American nuclear monopoly. The Chinese Communists came to power in the whole of mainland China and

North Korea attempted to conquer South Korea (1950). The Cold War was heating up to a point at which the adjective "cold" was losing validity.

Stalin's death coincided with a period of relaxation during which even a sworn cold warrior like Winston Churchill thought that the West should consider measures of détente. This opportunity, if it ever existed, was lost and the two nuclear giants developed their intercontinental ballistic missiles, some of which the Soviets, in their major exercise of effrontery, later placed in Cuba.

While Soviet policy, after the horrors of World War II, remained frozen in its ideological frame, American policy took an exhilarating leap into uncharted horizons. Old attitudes were superseded and old prejudices were overcome. The idea of active worldwide commitment replaced the traditional U.S. isolationism. This was not the result of the war alone. The United States had often shown a tendency to regard its wars as episodic interruptions to be succeeded by a reversion to a fortress mentality. That, after all, had happened after World War I. This time, by contrast, America understood that new technologies had destroyed its invulnerability. American foreign policy needed a new set of values which could only be expressed in a new vocabulary.

The Truman years are undoubtedly the constitutive period in the history of American Cold War diplomacy. Little substantive change was recorded until after the Vietnam War, and much of the conceptual thinking about international politics has become embedded in the national consciousness of the West ever since. The central themes were activism, leadership, responsibility, a wide vision of America's place in the world, and a particular emphasis on the vocation of America to uphold democracy against external and domestic threats.

The idea of America as the central pillar of an alliance with Western Europe as the main partner could not have been taken for granted when the Cold War began. It seemed to go against many of the traditions and prejudices of the American nation. Truman and Acheson may be said to have established this idea so firmly that a return to isolationism was effectively eliminated for all time.

One of the Truman administration's most important victories was won in the domestic domain. To have induced Republican party stalwarts such as Sen. Arthur H. Vandenberg to accept the principle of American worldwide involvement was Truman's most spectacular achievement. The wonder is that the authority for this revolutionary change was supplied by a President whose previous career had been restricted to parochial concerns, with no illumination of the sort that comes from extensive travel and immersion in the literature of international relations. It sounds strange to call Truman an intellectual revolutionary, but this would not be far from the truth.

If anything, the first U.S. reaction to the idea of worldwide involvement may have been excessively rhapsodic. A sense of recent disaster sometimes gives birth to lucid reason; but just as often it becomes sublimated into a messianic yearning for total, and therefore unattainable, perfection. There was more illusion than realism in the approach of leading statesmen immediately following World War II. The primary assumption was that the American, Soviet, and British victors would command the future; the ordeals that they had surmounted together would consecrate their partnership for future tasks. Soon, a whole cluster of hopes began to form around the central illusion of great power cooperation. It was assumed that the new system would give a large place to international organization. This time, there were no signs of the American isolationism which had caused the decline of the League of Nations. It seemed evident that the United Nations, unlike its hapless predecessor, would have the necessary armed forces to ensure respect for its decisions. How else could one explain why the three most powerful leaders in the world—Franklin D. Roosevelt, Joseph Stalin, and Winston

Churchill—had spent so many hours at Yalta in 1945 arguing about details of UN membership and voting procedures?

There was no end to the dream of a new and radiant dawn. International law would move from its peripheral status toward the center of the diplomatic discourse. Subject peoples would emerge in a steady evolution toward self-government. New levels of cooperation would ensure an expanding world economy; the key word here would be solidarity, not competition. As governments came to put more trust in each other and in international institutions, they would reduce their armaments, with consequent relief of political tensions and economic burdens. Diplomacy would be open, public, ecumenical, free of the conspiratorial atmosphere of the past and abundant in the production of agreements. Conflicting interests and ideologies would still exist, but they would be subdued by the overriding vision of a universal order. Even if the great powers did not share a common hope, they would surely be united by the common fear contained in the only eloquent sentence in the UN Charter—the fear of "the scourge of war, which twice in our lifetime has brought untold sorrow to mankind."[2]

Most of these forecasts would be refuted early in the first postwar decade. It may be questioned whether the immediate morrow of a traumatic experience is a good time to formulate new blueprints. The statesmen who planned the new era of international life were inspired by a shining vision which they somehow confused with reality. They assumed that a new story, never heard or told before, would unfold across the human scene. And this conviction about the new age was not held by naive idealists alone. It was shared by men of hard experience, nurtured in the wearying frustrations of conflict and war.

The Roosevelt White House had set the tone for naiveté in regard to great power cooperation. "We really believed," confessed Harry Hopkins, the President's friend and confidant, "that this was the dawn of the new day we had all been praying for and talking about for so many years. . . . The Russians had proved that they could be reasonable and farseeing and there wasn't any doubt in the minds of the President or any of us that we could live with them and get along with them peacefully for as far into the future as any of us could imagine. We were absolutely certain that we had won the first great victory of the peace."[3]

The emotion in the Roosevelt White House was too effusive. It should have been evident by the end of the war that the alliance between the Western powers and the Soviet Union had been a marriage of inconvenience, whose occasional courtesies concealed abrasive conflicts of interest and emotion.

The war in Europe had begun as a Western reaction to the brutal occupation of Eastern European states first by German and then by Soviet armies. In the Declaration on Liberated Europe of February 11, 1945, the Western powers and the Soviet Union had agreed that Poland should have "democratic institutions of [its] own choice."[4] But this promise was qualified by the Soviets' insistence that Poland have a government friendly to the Soviet Union. Moscow's interpretation was that "friendship" could only be secured if the Soviet Union had complete control over the policies of any Polish government.

In Moscow, U.S. Ambassador Averell Harriman thought he had achieved some gain by persuading Stalin to send his foreign minister, V. N. Molotov, to talk to President Truman in Washington. The idea that every difficult condition can be improved by high-level dialogue is one of the more persistent diplomatic delusions. When Molotov confronted Truman in the White House on May 26, 1945, it became evident that no situation is so bad that a badly conceived summit meeting cannot make it worse.

Molotov appealed to Russian vulnerability as the reason for seeking Soviet agreement on the composition of the Polish government. It is difficult to treat this theme without eloquence and emotion, but Molotov seems to have tried and succeeded.

Truman's response was rigorously formalistic. All that the Soviet Union had to do was to carry out the Yalta accord, agree to free elections in Poland, and accept the fortune of the result. Molotov said, "I have never been talked to like that in my life." Truman replied, "Carry out your agreements and you won't get talked to like that."[5]

In later years, when the Vietnam trauma inspired Americans with a pervasive instinct for self-criticism, a revisionist rift developed in the United States. Some hard questions were asked. Was Truman really justified in dealing so severely with Molotov's concerns about Russian insecurity? Was the Russian insistence on a defensive ring in Eastern Europe as preposterous as it appeared? Russia, after all, had suffered twenty million dead at the hands of the Germans. American losses had been less than half a million.

Each of the two great nations was the servant of its own history. While America, shielded by the Atlantic Ocean and British sea power, was expanding westward against weak resistance in a relatively empty continent, Russia was virtually defenseless against external attack from powerful European neighbors. The central theme of American history was security. The central theme of Russian history was fear.

The distrustful vision of a hostile world bent on the destruction of Russia was not invented by the Communist regime. It was an integral part of Russia's memory. In reacting to this threat the Communist leaders were following a normal thread of Russian experience. Communism never caused Russia to act in terms of its own security any differently than it would have acted under any regime after World War II. The ideology and rhetoric of communism determined how Russia explained its actions, but the actions themselves reflected a constant national experience. It was natural for Americans and the entire non-Communist world to feel that Russia was stretching its claim to security too far to be tolerated by Western minds, but it was unrealistic for America to hope that Russia would act as if it were America and accept the fortune of the dice in a Polish election.

American-Soviet rivalry, later known as the Cold War, was tragic in the classical sense; it was a Greek tragedy of compulsion, not a Christian tragedy of choice. The Russian demand to subjugate all its neighbors for the sake of its own security was something that Russia could not easily renounce—and which America could not possibly accept.

Nevertheless, the revisionist case which distributes blame for the Cold War evenly between the United States and the Soviet Union rests on thin ice. Moscow's ambitions went far beyond any legitimate concern about its boundaries with Eastern Europe. The Soviet Union aimed at the establishment of governments "friendly to the Soviet Union" first in Italy and France, and later in Poland, Czechoslovakia, Hungary, Cuba, Angola, Korea, and Afghanistan—together with a bid for superiority over the West in conventional weaponry, strategic equality in nuclear power, and acceptance of the Soviet claim to subvert democratic regimes all over the world. This did not sound much like a prescription for stability.

If great power cooperation was the most spectacular fallacy embraced after World War II, the myth of a powerful international organization was a close second. By 1946 it was clear that there was not going to be a UN force acting under the authority of the five major powers. It was simply not true that institutions would create a sense of world community. On the contrary, a sense of community would have to be created first, with effective international institutions as an ultimate consequence. Throughout the Cold War, the central actors in world politics would never cease to be nation-states claiming sovereignty in their external relations and giving international institutions a subsidiary role.

The fifty states that founded the United Nations did not even continue to be the main part of the world community. Over a hundred new sovereignties joined them in a great proliferation of independent states, many of them of minute dimensions. There were never "Five Great Powers" in any real sense. China grew in power but avoided detailed international involvement, and the special status accorded by the UN Charter to Britain and France was a chivalrous gesture to the past rather than a reflection of present reality. Germany and Japan developed an influence unforeseen by those who fashioned international institutions without them. Subject peoples came to independence not by the orderly evolution envisaged in the trusteeship provisions of the UN Charter but in a turbulent rush of changing winds.

Throughout the Cold War the world, far from engaging in disarmament, was caught up in an arms race of staggering scope. Not a single weapons system was abolished or reduced. The sterility of the arms control negotiations is astonishing when we consider some of the compulsions that ought to have worked in their favor. Celestial and infernal visions beyond Dante's imagination had entered the common thought and speech. The only early success of the disarmament movement was the treaty between the United States, Britain, and the USSR for the cessation of tests in the atmosphere, leaving all existing nuclear stockpiles intact. This was supplemented by the SALT treaty of 1972, which froze production of specified types of missiles without imposing ceilings on the number of warheads on strategic bombers. It was not until September 1996, well after the end of the Cold War, that a comprehensive treaty for the cessation of nuclear testing was concluded on President Bill Clinton's initiative in the United Nations.

International law did not celebrate a golden age during or even after the Cold War. Nations have preferred to resolve their conflicts by diplomacy, or even war, rather than submit their interests to legal adjudication. Diplomacy dislikes occasions in which any case can be completely lost. Throughout the Cold War, events had more power than ideas, and pragmatic interests, empirically defined, took precedence over written agreements. The "scourge of war" did not recur in its full range or scope, but many limited wars proved that military power was still a major element of international relations.

The cherished hope of creating international solidarities in what were optimistically called "nonpolitical" or "humanitarian" issues was frustrated by East-West and North-South rivalries. Regional institutions multiplied, but, with the important exception of the European Union, they have not succeeded in modifying national sovereignties through a meaningful degree of integration. The world is fragmenting and integrating at the same time.

And yet, without great power cooperation or a strong postwar peace organization, mankind has survived in a mood unanticipated in any blueprint. Global confrontation assumed many names, from "containment" through "Cold War" to "détente," but its contours changed little in five decades. The nuclear anguish created a new psychological context but did not lead to any enthusiasm for serious arms control. Limited wars were a sad but permanent feature of the international landscape during the Cold War period, but they seldom gave rise to apocalyptic visions of escalation or holocaust. Single "dominoes" managed to fall without bringing the international system to collapse. It was easier to diagnose the sickness of the world than to prescribe cures; and it was easier to prescribe cures than to persuade the patient to accept them.

Every Soviet exercise of brutal suppression was passively accepted by the world community. Baltic embassies in Washington were a subject of compassionate derision. Ostpolitik and the 1975 Helsinki Conference on Cooperation and Security in Europe were equivalent to the recognition of the global status quo created by the military realities of World War II. They were Soviet victories, but they could be absorbed by the West as phases in a prolonged trial of strength. It was tacitly agreed that neither the Communist nor the free world would impinge on the other's territory.

By the late 1980s the likelihood of military confrontation between East and West had greatly diminished. So much so that even allies and well-wishers of the United States questioned whether it was well advised in developing its Strategic Defense Initiative ("star wars") further. Yet it cannot be doubted that Soviet despair of keeping pace with audacious American technology was one of the calculations that drove Mikhail Gorbachev to perestroika, which began the unraveling of Soviet power.

Another American contribution to Soviet collapse was the head-on assault by the Reagan administration against all pro-Soviet regimes without concern for their ideological preferences. The only criterion for winning American aid was a candidate's anti-Soviet policy. The United States would make common cause with democratic entities such as the Polish Solidarity movement, or with Islamic fundamentalists such as the Afghan mujahidin, for whose doctrines most Americans had no sympathy. In the Middle East the United States would find reason to strengthen Israeli democracy but would also embrace the theocratic rulers of Saudi Arabia and Kuwait. The motto in Washington was, "The enemy of my enemy is my friend." Concern for democratic ideals and human rights had no place in a system of thought and feeling in which anti-Sovietism was the sole credential for U.S. support.

The collapse of the Soviet Union could not have occurred without an irrepressible urge for innovation within the Soviet republics. In historical terms, the principal architect of change was Gorbachev. His ambition was to reform the Communist system, not to destroy it, but once embarked on the reformist course he saw it run away from his control. By that time a new, liberalizing spirit had put the option of brutal suppression out of reach. The possibility of a successful defense of the Soviet empire had disappeared.

Those who lived in Europe as the Cold War subsided will not easily forget the intense surprise that greeted Gorbachev's arrival in the capitals that had winced and cringed before the overpowering might of the Soviet colossus. His personal demeanor announced that the Soviet Union had become a different reality than anything that had been known about Russia before. His unbearable loquacity was the only attribute that he shared with his predecessors. But this was offset by the startling change that he brought to the image of the Soviet leadership in Europe and beyond. His correct Western tailoring, his enunciation of ideas from the world of self-determination and liberalism, the fashionably European appearance of his wife, and the lack of bluster and arrogance in his discourse all proclaimed that the Soviet Union and its constituent republics had decided to become Europeans in most connotations of that term.

Seweryn Bialer has explained this cogently in the context of the 1991 coup against Gorbachev: "Perestroika created the conditions that made it impossible for the [pro-Communist] coup to succeed. Those who acted against Gorbachev believed that intimidation would still be decisive, as it had been for decades. The hoary clique could not see that much of the Soviet population had finally overcome its fear. Tanks on the streets were no longer enough."[6]

It is true that Boris Yeltsin became famous by standing on a tank and defying the Soviet regime, but he could not have maintained that posture if Gorbachev had not created the atmosphere in which the Russian soldiers felt bound to abstain from ejecting him.

Among the external forces that pushed the Soviet Union on its road to disintegration, pride of place must belong to the communications revolution. The Soviet government began with a feeble effort to limit the diffusion of computers, printers, and fax machines, but its military interests would have been crippled by the suppression of these new technologies. As these spread across the world, it became evident that the days of closed societies were numbered. The rigid Soviet system would have to compete with the free world for popular support. All the ingredients of free communities, from movies, newspapers, and television to rock music and jeans, penetrated Moscow, St. Petersburg, and the cities of Ukraine. Authority, even when exercised in the Russian Federation by Boris Yeltsin without much regard for conciliatory method, is subject to the humbling influences of electoral politics. Russia is neither egalitarian nor liberal, but it has come far from the nightmare conditions characteristic of all the regimes from Stalin to Brezhnev.

The Western alliance is beginning to grasp that the end of the Cold War is not necessarily the same as the dawn of a new international order. For the rest of the 1990s and beyond, the diplomatic scene will be marked by tension, complexity, and paradox. The nuclear era is not over, as developments in some Third World countries prove, but the prospect of planetary annihilation has been reduced to close to the vanishing point. On the other hand, the amount of misery, starvation, refugee flight, and violence exceeds what most nations had expected after the democratic triumphs of the early nineties.

With a million dead in the Rwanda tragedy and two hundred thousand in the avoidable Bosnian war, it is idle to assert that the world has made good use of the Communist eclipse.

Paradoxically, the Cold War ended as it began—with the potential conduct of Russia as the main source of European disquiet. The elections in the summer of 1996 leading to Yeltsin's victory were an astonishing innovation. Russians lining up to go to the polling stations and accepting the verdict of ballot boxes— could anything be more unlikely than this?

In this perspective, the Russian elections are a huge success for democracy. At this writing, however, all of Russia's neighbors have a sense of insecurity about their future. The violent suppression of Chechnya's bid for independence exposed the fragility of the federal structure. Russia is still, in Churchill's phrase, "a riddle wrapped in a mystery inside an enigma"[7]—but without the cosmic implications of the Cold War era.

The Western consciousness of the Cold War was first articulated by the generation's most eloquent voice: "From Stettin in the Baltic to Trieste in the Adriatic, an iron curtain has descended across the Continent. Behind that line lie all the capitals of the ancient states of Central and Eastern Europe. Warsaw, Berlin, Prague, Vienna, Budapest, Belgrade, Bucharest and Sofia . . . all are subject in one form or another, not only to Soviet influence but to a very high and, in many cases, increasing measure of control from Moscow. . . . Police governments are prevailing in nearly every case."[8]

The remarkable fact is that Churchill's symphonic utterance at Fulton, Missouri, on March 5, 1946, was ungraciously criticized at the time in America and in many parts of Europe. It was regarded as an unwelcome intrusion of reality into the more enticing world of wistful fantasy. It was, in fact, the naked truth resonantly expressed.

The least expected prospect was that all the capitals sonorously recited by Churchill would now be free republics seeking their place in the North Atlantic Treaty Organization and the European Union.

The half-century of the Cold War was "life on the brink." The coming chapters will reveal that on more than one occasion there was a real chance that nuclear weapons would be used, thus opening a Pandora's box in response to relatively minor strategic contingencies. Today, the nuclear projects in Iran, Iraq, and North Korea forbid the facile conclusion that the atomic weapons age is conclusively ended. But its main terrors are behind us.

Yet the post–Cold War—with its mounting record of affliction, the question mark hanging over North Korea, China, Iran,
Rwanda, Somalia, Chechnya, and Haiti, its refugee tragedies and
monstrous "ethnic cleansings," its subordination of human rights
to tyrannical despotisms and commercial expediencies—is evidently an era with no clear moral certainties. Yet its sufferings,
poignant as they still are, pale in comparison to the relief of
knowing that the planet itself is saved from self-destruction and
that new prospects of peace are waiting to unfold.

The professional diplomatic community emerges from the
Cold War with a record of restraint and control in an era when
those qualities were in greatest need. In a world of more than
185 states, the number of potential armed conflicts has been far
greater than the number of those that have actually erupted into
violence. In a world that once had fifty thousand nuclear warheads, the fact that such weaponry has never again been used,
despite the vehemence of interpower conflicts, entitles the diplomacy of the Cold War period to be accounted an overwhelming
success.

One of the embarrassing facts about American foreign policy
has been its propensity for self-disguise. American statesmen and
academics, under the Wilsonian spell, have constantly described
their policies in terms opposed to their reality. U.S. rhetoric has
always condemned "spheres of influence, alliances and balances
of power." But these words effectively describe the very policies
that the United States has actually implemented. Its attitude toward Guatemala, the Dominican Republic, Panama, Grenada,
and even Cuba is explicable only on the assumption that the
United States views the Latin American continent as a "sphere of
influence." The NATO commitment has much of the rhetoric
and a great deal of the trappings of an "alliance." And the entire
thrust and philosophy of the American defense policy has been
squarely rooted in the "balance of power" idea.

George F. Kennan, the prophet of American realism, admitted

that the best way of dealing with Russia was through a reasonable balance of power and understanding on spheres of influence. He wrote: "I continued . . . to be an advocate . . . of a prompt and clear recognition of the division of Europe into spheres of influence."[9] Such advocacy was bound to be audacious and lonely, since "balance of power" and "spheres of influence" are forbidden phrases in the idealistic American vocabulary, however consistently they are applied in American practice.

The alternative to a balance of power is an imbalance of power which has usually provoked wars and has never consolidated peace. In a world that is still not governed by a universally accepted law, statesmen will usually have to compromise between what justice demands and what circumstances permit.

The formal end of the Cold War was celebrated in Paris on May 27, 1997, when the NATO signatories concluded an agreement with Russia. The seven major industrialized countries became popularly known as the "Eight."

The Russian economy was far less prosperous than those of most other NATO members, but the rhetoric at Paris was understandably rhapsodic. There was a strong temptation to accentuate the contrast between past and present. NATO had been the most successful alliance in world history. It had deterred the Soviet Union from explosive adventure when Russian forces had been capable of shattering the European equilibrium and igniting a conflict of horrendous scope. All the metaphors of reconciliation were too weak to describe the sudden transition from the dark foreboding of the mid-1950s to the new age of international consensus that seemed to be aglow on an early horizon.

Boris Yeltsin as the president of the new Russia made the most of his celebratory opportunities as he strode, beaming with pride, into the company of those whom he had recently regarded as the adversaries of his flag.

Yet there was no honeymoon atmosphere in Denver, Colorado, when the Seven first decided to become the Eight. The Western powers were asking themselves searching questions. Was it not true that NATO counsels were confused? Was it insignificant that Russian forces were still occupying territories in the sovereign areas of Georgia and Estonia while the West and Russia were at daggers drawn in their policies for Iran and Iraq? True, the West no longer believed that Russia and China belonged to the same "Terrorist International," but could it rely on its own capacity to reconcile its traditions of human rights with the need to accept the realities of the new Russian Federation?

There was also an anxious semantic discussion. Was it realistic to believe that Russia would be a docile member of the new team? Was Russia not liable to wield a veto over the major table at which Russian-American relationships would evolve?

The Western powers ended, as so often in their history, with a decision to transcend their anxieties by hopeful rhetoric. With Poland, Hungary, and the Czech Republic entering the NATO alliance in the full panoply of membership, there was no time to ask the awkward questions. These included how the NATO powers would react if Russia exercised pressure on Poland and Ukraine and how the Baltic countries would line up if Russian occupying troops maintained an unwanted presence in the recently liberated Baltic states.

The mood became more somber with every passing day. Perhaps the answer would be simply to limit the number of days in which discussion would be open?

The solemn conclave ended with a statement that it "expect[ed]" Russia to desist from all pressures and threats in Europe.

Diplomats touch nothing that they do not adjourn.

2 Dilemmas of Diplomats

*People who respond to international affairs divide temperamentally
into two schools: those who first ask of a policy, "Is it morally right?"
and those who first ask, "Will it work?"; those who see policies as
good or evil, and those who see them as wise or foolish. One cannot
presume an ultimate metaphysical antagonism between the moralist
and the realist. No realist can wholly escape perceptions of good and
evil, and no policy can wholly divorce ethical from geopolitical
considerations.* —Arthur M. Schlesinger, Jr.

Diplomacy is as old as the history of mankind, but the ethical
dilemmas of diplomats do not come into conspicuous view until
the early part of the twentieth century. In ancient and medieval
times diplomats were singularly free from ethical torment. It took
two world wars with fifty million deaths, a horrifying toll of
maimed and wounded, a vast spread of devastation in Europe, a
genocidal Holocaust of European Jews, and the spectacle of two
ravaged cities in Japan to persuade public opinion that war and
peace are not a specialized concern of generals and soldiers alone.
After World War II, it dawned on humanity that if war is everybody's tragedy, peace must be everybody's business. In the light of
this new consciousness it was no longer feasible to leave the
negotiation of disputes to experts.

The very existence of nuclear weapons, deliberately pointing
at great cities, made it impossible to subordinate the prevention
of war to any other consideration. Diplomatic decisions hence-

forth were invested with a tension and solemnity that had never been known before.

Politics has been described as "the arena where power and conscience meet, and will be meeting until the end of time."[1] Until the modern age, the victory of power over conscience was beyond dispute. The founders of all the diplomatic traditions followed the example brutally formulated by the Athenians when they prepared to massacre the inhabitants of the island of Melos: "The strong do what they can and the weak suffer what they must."[2]

Nevertheless, it was a Greek statesman who argued a more pragmatic case. The celebrated orator Demosthenes described the ambassadorial function in words that today's envoys could usefully take to heart: "Ambassadors have no battleships at their disposal, or heavy infantry, or fortresses; their weapons are words and opportunities. In important transactions opportunities are fleeting; once they are missed they cannot be recovered. It is a greater offense to deprive a democracy of an opportunity than it would be thus to deprive an oligarchy or an autocracy."[3]

Greek senates and assemblies, after listening to rhetoric, reacted no differently than modern audiences. François de Callières, the advisor to Louis XIV, in his majestic treatise on negotiation, discusses the response of the Spartan leaders to the verbosity of a visiting mission from the island of Samos: "We have forgotten the beginning of your harangue; we paid no heed to the middle of it, and nothing has given us pleasure in it except the end."[4]

The Greek city-states are rightly regarded as the primary architects of diplomatic traditions. Diplomacy flourishes best in conditions of fragmentation, pluralism, and theoretical equality of status among its component parts. In such conditions, without any unit claiming superiority over others, it is possible to achieve goals only by persuasion, eloquence, inducement, threats, and— if need be—intimidation. The ancient Greeks lived in a multistate system and they bequeathed a refined vocabulary of diplomatic terms such as "truces," "alliances," "commercial accords," "conventions," and even "peace." Arbitration was a common recourse for this litigious people and there are records of at least fifty arbitration agreements between Greek states. Ideological subtleties had no place in the Greek system. None of the cities had such an ardent devotion to its own political system as to encourage it to convert other cities by missionary zeal.

The ideology of the Greek cities was patriotism; they "regarded all other Hellenes as potential enemies, and all barbarians as natural slaves."[5] Barbarians was the name given to all those who did not speak the Greek language.

Despite these disagreeable qualities, the egotism of the Hellenes was tempered by restraint, which they attributed to divine revelation under the tutelage of Zeus but which secular thinking would regard as good common sense. Some of these inhibitions even had a humanitarian slant, such as those that forbade unheralded and undeclared war and crimes against prisoners.

When the Greeks left the center of history, their Roman successors never questioned the need to coerce foreigners to accept the *Pax Romana* while crushing all opposition. Foreign ambassadors to imperial Rome never went home with agreeable recollections. They had to pass suspicious scrutiny before obtaining the right of entry, had to wait for long periods before addressing the Senate, were lodged in rat-infested buildings, and were "encouraged" to leave with all possible dispatch. Courtesy to foreigners was not the distinguishing feature of imperial Rome.

Nor did it characterize the twelfth-century Byzantine courts, which made themselves unpopular by using ambassadors for espionage as well as for the gathering of information. Envoys to the Byzantine courts were instructed to speak nothing but words of praise to the governments of their accreditation. Obsequiousness was not discouraged. The major effort of the Byzantine leaders was to give an impression of their own overwhelming military power. This was always achieved, but seldom by honest methods. Ambassadors to Constantinople were expected to attend interminable military reviews at which the same troops would enter the city by one gate and emerge from another, coming round and round again several times, carrying different types and colors of uniforms and armor.

The adversarial atmosphere surrounding diplomacy was displayed by the Ottoman Turkish sultans, who required ambassadors to be bound hand and foot before entering the royal presence and to kiss the sultan's robe. It is hard to understand why sane men aspired to these posts.

Italy was the first country to accord resident status to ambassadors, but the emissaries had to respect the sacred egoism of their sovereigns. One of the earliest literary commentators on diplomacy, Ermolao Barbara, says, quite explicitly, that "the duty of the ambassador is to do, say, advise, and think whatever may best serve the preservation and the aggrandizement of his own state." The state and the state alone is the judge of what its own vital interests are and how they may best be protected.

Little changed until recent times. The supreme ethic of a diplomat has been "my country, right or wrong." As in many other instances, the French found an elegant way of expressing a questionable idea. They called it *raison d'état*.

The origins of diplomacy are rooted in the acceptance of rivalry as the natural condition of interstate relations, and diplomats have always had to be singleminded in defending their national interest against all others. Niccolò Machiavelli, who had diplomatic experience in the service of his Florentine prince, was merely more candid than his contemporaries in the sharpness with which he separated the morality of power from individual ethics. In his *Discourses* he emphasizes that the standards whereby people measure the morality of an individual cannot apply to the acts of the state. Conduct that would be regarded as sinful in any religious context, such as cheating, stealing, killing, or lying, might be accepted and even praised when performed in the name of the state. On the issue of raison d'état Machiavelli is emphatic and unreserved: "For where the very safety of the country depends upon the resolution to be taken, no considerations of justice or injustice, humanity or cruelty, nor of glory or of shame, should be allowed to prevail. But putting all other considerations aside, the only question should be, What course will save the life and liberty of the country?"[6]

This does not convict Machiavelli of conscious immorality. He was courageous enough to make a strong case for the thesis that there are two moralities. He regarded it as a noble and, therefore, a moral attitude to hope for the restoration of a society such as the Athens of Pericles, the Florence of the Renaissance, or the Rome of the Principate, governed by a ruling class of brave, intelligent, resourceful, gifted men who knew how to seize opportunities and put them to use. But he stressed that if that is your aim, you must understand that you cannot attain it by what he called "Christian virtues" such as humility, acceptance of suffering, unworldliness, and the hope of salvation in an afterlife.

The most penetrating insight of Machiavelli, that states do not and should not act like individuals in society, finds secular expression hundreds of years later in the adherents to the realist school of American diplomacy, which defends the "custodian" theory. Their reasoning is that statesmen are charged with no more than the temporary trusteeship of assets and interests that are not their own. It was a spiritual leader, Reinhold Niebuhr, who declared that statesmen must be more scrupulous in defense of national interests than of personal advantage. "Unselfishness," he says, "is inappropriate to the action of a state. No one has a right to be unselfish with other people's interests."[7] In short, the individual's duty of self-sacrifice and the state's duty of self-preservation are often in conflict.

In all the ages after Machiavelli leaders and spokesmen of states have been unable to escape from a moral predicament. Diplomats at all levels operate in a world of competing sovereignties in which it is not easy to uphold uncompromising morality. Indeed, it is not until the eighteenth century that we find a moralistic definition of the duties of diplomats. This was when Hugo Grotius, the Dutch jurist, invoked what he called "a sense of justice and of right reason" as the motive for interstate cooperation. The growing diplomatic community was the trustee of this new secular ideal, and behind the shield of its immunities it developed a deepening sense of solidarity.

The professional status of diplomacy only became firm in 1626, when Cardinal Richelieu, as diplomatic advisor to Louis XIII, established a Ministry of External Affairs to centralize the management of foreign relations under a single roof. The practice was followed all over Europe, where French diplomatic leadership was now generally recognized in every sphere, including the recognition of French as the vernacular of diplomacy. But Richelieu is correctly described by modern writers as believing that national interest, not idealism, must prevail in the world of diplomacy. In the words of one of Richelieu's eminent admirers, "In an age still dominated by religious zeal and ideological fanaticism, a dispassionate foreign policy free of moral imperatives stood out like a snow-covered Alp in the desert. Richelieu's . . . only criterion in making alliances was that they served France's interests. . . . Fate had made him a prince of the Church . . . opportunity had enabled him to transform the international order to the vast advantage of his country."[8]

In the nineteenth century, after the Napoleonic Wars, diplomacy entered its period of grace. For exactly a century, between 1815 and 1914, war was marginal and peace seemed to be the normal condition of mankind. Stability was maintained through the informal but effective system of the Concert of Europe. It was a remarkable achievement. Peace was secured for long periods in an age in which war aroused no moral revulsion. War had not ceased to be regarded as a legitimate and appropriate instrument of policy, and the rationality of peace was not moral or legal; it was entirely pragmatic. The European system responded to the enlightened self-interest of the major powers: Austro-Hungary, Britain, France, Prussia, Russia, and the Ottoman Empire. All the sovereigns of that period considered that the maintenance of the existing balance offered greater power and safety than could be obtained by its disruption.

Whenever rivalry became too intense, the major powers would compensate each other at the expense of the territories and peoples in which there were no recognized sovereign states. Colonialism was quite legitimate in the theory and practice of the nineteenth-century international system. When France was disgruntled, after its defeat in 1870 and 1871, the German prince Otto von Bismarck feared that the cooperation of France with the Concert of Europe would be fragile unless the French received some redress or consideration. He simply urged France to annex Tunisia. This solution was not ethically inspiring, but it worked.

The habit of insuring European stability by diverting expansionist ambitions into Africa and Asia continued well into this century. When the leaders of France and Britain met Benito Mussolini at the Stresa Conference in 1935, their decision to accept his aggression in Ethiopia was directly related to their hope of keeping Italy as a satisfied member of the European system.

The Concert of Europe had admirable features, but it cannot be praised for ethical motivation. The aim of diplomacy in the nineteenth century was European stability, not universal equality. And this aim was achieved. It was an era in which power and responsibility, force and interests were brought into harmony. Economic and technological progress, together with the proven durability of peace, created a utopian mystique. The Scottish immigrant to America Andrew Carnegie, in establishing his foundation, gave his researchers simple advice: "Begin by solving the problem of war and, once that is settled, go on to something else."

It would soon become clear that the problem of war was far

from "settled," but there was enough success in the promotion of stability to give diplomats a sense of achievement. In France, Britain, Italy, and other European states, diplomacy emerged as a distinguished vocation with specialized professional skills and a particular appeal to social and intellectual elites.

The most decisive innovation in the nineteenth century was the end of the European monopoly through the entry of the United States into the small group of senior members in the diplomatic community. It is easy to forget how slow and reluctant this process was. In its early formative years, America would have preferred not to have a foreign policy at all. The New World was obsessed with the ecstasy of separation from the Old. Its electorate constantly celebrated the joys of distance. The central purpose of American life was to put the European experience behind, especially the memories of conflicts and wars. The first definition of American foreign interests was suspicious and restrictive: "the business of America with Europe [is] commerce, not politics or war," said John Adams.[9]

The American Revolution had engendered a sharp suspicion of external entanglements. Most of the Founding Fathers shared the austere view of Adams: "I confess I have sometimes thought that after a few years, it will be the best thing we could do to recall every minister from Europe and send embassies only on special occasions."

Others echoed a common view, not completely eradicated up to our own times, that those who represented their countries at war might easily forget whence they came and fall under the seduction of alien ideas. John Quincy Adams insisted that diplomats should always be recalled after a few years, "to be renovated by the wholesome republican atmosphere of their own country."

American success was measured by the growth of domestic resources and welfare; external affairs were distractions to be dealt with as summarily as possible. There was also the fact that foreign affairs meant involvement in Europe, and this evoked the oldest and deepest reservations in American political thought. "Why," exclaimed George Washington in his Farewell Address, "forego the advantages of so peculiar a situation? . . . Why, by interweaving our destiny with that of any part of Europe, entangle our peace and prosperity in the toils of European Ambition, Rivalship, Interest, Humor or Caprice?"[10]

In strictly objective terms these references to Europe were churlish and unfounded. America was able to expand and flourish within its continental expanse because the balance of power in Europe neutralized America against any hostile European intrusion, while British naval supremacy ensured the freedom of the seas without laying any burden on the United States. Remote from the compromises and exigencies of power politics, Americans have been able to comment on international affairs in a detached, moralistic tone. American foreign policy was, in the main, a series of reactions to emergencies provoked from outside. When a "clear and present danger" had been dealt with, the United States would return to domestic concerns.

It would be a mistake to regard American isolationism as a thing of the distant past, a memory of the pastoral folklore of the early years. The Neutrality Acts were adopted in 1935–37, not in some prehistoric past. The speed with which Americans insisted on "bringing the boys back home" before reaping the fruits of victory in World War II and after the Gulf War reflected a rooted tendency of Americans to see foreign involvement as an episodic interruption of their normal national rhythm, not as a destiny that would have to accompany them into an indefinite future.

In 1906 the United States had only nine embassies abroad, the rest being legations. A century earlier, President Thomas Jefferson had asked the Congress to insure that "there should be someone in the department of State when the secretary was out for lunch." The number of those enrolled in the Foreign Service of the United States, up to the end of World II, was less than eight hundred, and fewer than half of the serving heads of missions were career diplomats. The requirements of the foreign policy establishment were uniformly modest and tentative.

World War I was less massive in its lethal effects than World War II, but it was quite sufficient to shake diplomacy out of its moral neutrality. The traumatic effects of the first war gave American policy a cautious, reserved, but perceptible entry into the world's diplomatic discourse. But the war itself left no proud memories behind. The United States' role was enacted late in the war and on a limited scale compared with the sacrifices of France and Britain. It was not convincing to call it an American victory.

By contrast, America was unprecedentedly dominant in the diplomacy of the post–World War I period. It was from America that the first frank and resonant call was heard in defense of the idea that diplomacy has an essentially moral basis. The new voice was that of President Woodrow Wilson, calling for open covenants, an end to coercive regimes, a liberation of peoples from traditional servitudes, and an international system based on the principle of self-determination.

Wilsonianism has entered the international vocabulary as the expression of the idealistic theme in the international outlook of the United States and other Western democracies. "The new things in the world," Wilson proclaimed on June 5, 1914, "are the things that are divorced from force. They are the moral compulsions of the human conscience. No man can turn away from these things without turning away from the hope of all the world. . . . The United States," he proudly declared, "have not the distinction of being masters of the world, but the distinction of carrying certain lights for the world that the world has never so distinctly seen before."[11]

The massive echoes of Wilson's voyage to Europe are reflected in the description by the British diplomatic historian Harold

Nicolson, who was present at the peace conference over which Wilson presided in 1919:

> The one thing which rendered Wilsonianism so passionately interesting at the moment was the fact that this centennial dream was suddenly backed by the overwhelming resources of the strongest Power in the world. Here was a man who represented the greatest physical force which had ever existed and who had pledged himself openly to the most ambitious moral theory which any statesman had ever pronounced. It was not that the ideas of Woodrow Wilson were so apocalyptic: it was that for the first time in history you had a man who possessed, not the desire merely, not the power alone, but the unquestioned opportunity to enforce these ideas upon the whole world. We should have been insensitive indeed had we not been inspired by the magnitude of such an occasion.[12]

Wilson's role in enunciating the moral themes of international relations has been so emphatic that seven decades later we find Henry Kissinger writing: "It is above all to the drumbeat of Wilsonian idealism that American foreign policy has marched since his watershed presidency and continues to march to this day."[13]

My own impression is that Wilsonian idealism dominates the rhetoric but not the policies of the United States. All American and most other governments take their decisions in terms of national interest and explain their decisions in terms of self-sacrificial altruism.

In the same book, Kissinger traced the defects and limitations of the Wilsonian idea back to the time of Washington: "As the repository of the principle of liberty, America found it natural to interpret the security conferred on it by great oceans, as a sign of divine providence, and to attribute its actions to superior moral insight instead of to a margin of security not shared by any other nation."[14]

If this analysis is true, it follows that the United States has not been more virtuous than other nations. It has only been more fortunate.

Wilson's idealism did not come to effective expression in the peace conference over which he presided, or in the League of Nations which he fathered. He died sadly amid the debris of his own vision. He had pleaded for self-determination but said, regretfully, "I never knew that there were a million Germans in Bohemia." Not to have known this is to have shared responsibility for World War II. The role of ignorance in the guidance of great decisions deserves more consideration than it has received.

In his first presidency, Wilson had invaded Mexico to the sound of his own rather sanctimonious announcement that he was doing this "for the benefit of mankind." Having enunciated his belief in "open covenants," he had organized the most conspiratorial, secretive peace conference in world history, in whose decisions the principle of self-determination was blatantly violated in many crucial areas. A contemporary observer noted, "[Wilson] and his conscience were on terms of such incessant intimacy that any little disagreement between them could easily be arranged. . . . The active belief that God, Wilson and the People would triumph in the end . . . led him to look upon his own inconsistencies as mere transient details in the one great impulse toward right and justice."[15]

Yet, the promulgation of Wilson's moralistic theme was so sensational in its time that the union between Wilsonianism and the idea of international idealism is historically justified. But Wilsonianism and realism have been in head-on conflict. The world is composed, politically and juridically, of nation-states, and here was the American leader calling for them to behave in a way in which nation-states had never behaved in the whole of human history. The central theme of that history is that the loyalties, passions, and allegiances which men devote to their own nations are not transferrable to any idea of world community. When

Americans landed on the moon, they planted their own stars and stripes on that bleak landscape, not a portrayal of planet Earth.

The confrontation between power and conscience is enacted today in a very wide range of decisions and actions. I shall allude to five themes in which the confrontation has been sharp and distinct.

First: The fear of nuclear war may have preserved mankind. But can it ever be right to use a weapon which would destroy the resources and beauties of the Earth as well as the values that it purports to defend? And if it is not morally right to use nuclear warheads, can it be right to threaten their use?

Second: Nonnuclear wars have not ceased as a result of the nuclear terror. They have even proliferated because the danger of escalation to nuclear proportions no longer exists.

Third: The United Nations Charter enthrones human rights as a principle of international concern. Is it possible to reconcile that concern with the doctrine of state sovereignty on which the international equilibrium depends?

Fourth: Until the end of World War II, the world was divided between the few nations enjoying sovereignty and the mass of humanity that was subjugated to imperial powers. This has been an affront to the conscience as well as to the interests of mankind. Self-determination has won unprecedented gains.

Fifth: Although juridical inequalities between nations have been largely overcome, there are vast gaps in economic opportunity and in access to the fruits of science, technology, and education. These gaps threaten international stability and are ethically dubious.

Another difficulty is inherent in the very idea of international representation. Diplomacy has developed across the centuries as a sacred calling requiring early discipleship and constant devotion. Since the ambassador is often distant from his (or her) country and thrown into close contact with people from other lands, he tends to develop a closer affinity with his professional colleagues than with his fellow citizens at home. He is very vulnerable. On the one hand, he is an authoritative champion of his country's interests; indeed, his basic function is to get as much as possible for his country while giving as little as possible in return. But he is more obliged than any other public servant to perceive the limitation of national attitudes and to seek legitimacy for his positions in terms of a broader universal ideal.

Domestic opinion is liable to make the diplomat the scapegoat for the nation's inability to get its own way. Since governments are usually constituted with an eye on domestic policy, the public expects a link of consequence between what a government decides and what ensues from that decision. In international life no such automatic consequence is possible, since the power and sovereignty of the state do not extend into the external realm.

The diplomat is the bearer of a view of the outside world which his fellow citizens cannot always follow or accept. The task of peacemaking demands the intellectual gift of seeing all around a problem, leaving no element out of account, and estimating all the elements in their relative proportions. It requires the moral gift of an attitude that favors compromise, the taking of long views, and working for distant ends. None of these attitudes is congenial to immediate political advantage.

Foreign policy is intrinsically "foreign," that is, remote from the intimate consciousness of the people. The diplomat faces the ordeal of alienation. With the growing number and diversity of states goes a deeper schism between politics, traditions, and cultures.

If it is inequitable and fruitless to ask why diplomats have not prevented war, it is more legitimate to ask why they never seem to give warning of its eruption. Here we face an extraordinary record of strategic surprise. There seems to be something built into the international consciousness that prevents it from foreseeing that which becomes self-evident in retrospect. Much of the public's resentment against the world diplomatic community arises from the failure of diplomacy, even when allied with military intelligence, to protect the international system from the shock of surprise. Despite the communications revolution and the license which diplomatic practice now allows to those seeking information in foreign countries, the hard fact is that there is much more surprise than foresight in the international history of this century.

The Soviet Union suffered surprise when invaded by Germany. So did the United States when its fleet was destroyed at Pearl Harbor.

The United States was again surprised when North Korea invaded South Korea, and subsequently when China intervened decisively in the Korean War.

Israel was surprised by the sudden blockade and troop movements initiated by Egypt under President Gamal Abdel Nasser in May 1967. A few weeks later Egypt was surprised by the intensity of Israel's response.

Before World War II Britain had been surprised by the Soviet-German pact leading to the attack on Poland and the expansion of the conflict. The United States was surprised by the crises precipitated by the Soviet Union over Iran in 1946 and Berlin in 1948, 1958, 1959, and 1961, and especially by the Soviet introduction of missiles into Cuba in 1962.

Israel was surprised by the Egyptian and Syrian attack on October 6, 1973. Egypt was surprised by the crossing of the Suez Canal by Israeli forces, which enabled Israel to recuperate from the Egyptian assault on Yom Kippur 1973.

All the Western powers were surprised by the landing of Turkish troops on Cyprus in 1974 and by the Soviet-Cuban intervention in the Angolan civil war in 1975.

The French military leaders were surprised by the violence of the German tank breakthrough in May 1940. The Soviet Union had been surprised by the success of the Finnish resistance to the Soviet attack in the Winter War of 1939–40.

The explanation of this extraordinary record of surprises does not lie in inaccurate information. In every case the physical facts about troop concentrations and political hostility were known and often documented in the media. Yet those who were threatened by them lent themselves easily to lenient interpretations. In a few cases there was successful disinformation, as in the summer of 1973, when Egypt spread many stories about its weakness and unpreparedness in the hope that Israel and others would not regard its troop concentrations in October as proof of imminent assault.

But a deeper cause for surprise lies in the psychological structure of governments and statesmen. Their habit is to formulate appraisals of enemy intentions and capacities and then to reject any prediction that contradicts their sacred texts. There is also a tendency to believe that habits of an adversary in the past are bound to arise in the future. Thus American intelligence services initially refused to believe that the Soviet Union was installing missiles in Cuba because, in previous years, Moscow had scrupulously avoided placing missiles in situations in which they could threaten U.S. targets and invite reaction by the United States, which had a clear superiority of power.

Similarly, Israeli intelligence declined to believe that Egyptian troop concentrations in October 1973 were auguries of war because similar troop concentrations in May 1973 had not led to war.

The influence of experience and analogy in the training of diplomats may well mean that they will not be alert for the original, unpredictable, innovative factors in international conduct. The significant elements in human experience are to be found not in those domains in which events are similar to each other but in those where they are particular and unique.

Another difficulty arises from the fact that the mere accumulation of arms no longer signifies aggressive intent. The arms control dilemma is far less central to the ethical issue than was once commonly believed. Arms are more a result than a cause of international tension. Nations do not make war because they have arms. They have arms because they believe that they might be provoked or tempted into making war.

So long as nations compete in the power balance, the hope of massive disarmament will be pushed into a corner. It is evident that the tensions created or aggravated by arms races can only be solved, if at all, within a broader context of political settlement. Arms control debates, with their narrow application to categories and quantities of weapons, will have no more than marginal effects.[16]

The principle of equality is served within nation-states by taxation systems which transfer resources from the wealthy to the indigent sectors of society. In international life there is no such mandatory obligation and the issue is left to the voluntary action of the few states which choose to dispense foreign aid.

This implies a degree of romantic chivalry which reaches extreme expression in statements like that of the social theorist Kenneth Boulding, who writes that "people in Maine should feel the same degree of responsibility toward the people of Japan and Chile as they feel toward California."

Whatever it is that people "should feel," the fact is that there are very few even in the most enlightened societies who are capable of projecting their sense of obligation so far afield. Practical statesmanship avoids this hyperbole and rests the case for foreign aid on grounds of common humanity or international stability. That was the approach followed by the Brandt and Pearson commissions,[17] both headed by eminent statesman of liberal bent who investigated the problems of international aid. They did not moralize or preach; they did make a strong case for the idea that states can injure each other by their weakness and not only by their strength, so that an impoverished region living on the outskirts of an affluent area can have the same disruptive effects as a slum in the vicinity of a prosperous town.

These reports suggested the globalization of international aid development under principles that would give greater power to international institutions and to developing countries. They lingered at length on the huge sums spent on armaments, thus endorsing the somewhat naive assumption that if money were saved on armaments, it would somehow end up being devoted to development projects in poor countries.

The wealthy countries have admittedly been confused in their Third World policies and this failure has worked against a harmonious international consensus. But the new states have contributed to deadlock and mutual alienation. They have relied on the delusion that resolutions of international agencies couched in coercive and condemnatory terms are an adequate substitute for courteous and patient diplomacy. They have presented themselves without convincing evidence as the embodiment of the universal conscience, purer and freer from sin than ordinary mortals and governments. They have evaded their own share of responsibility by placing the whole charge for the problem and its solution on the outside world and blaming the old colonial systems for their own deficiencies.

Most countries in the Third World do not offer the other two worlds many social visions worthy of envy or emulation. The record on human rights in the Third World is often poor, and sometimes horrific. Idi Amin in Uganda, "Emperor" Jean Bedel Bokassa in the Central African Republic, and Pol Pot in Cambodia (Kampuchea) would enter the list of revolting tyrannies in any age.

At the Helsinki Conference of 1975 the human rights question was focused mainly on the Soviet Union, but there was more brutality in the Third World dictatorships than in the Soviet Union. Not because the Soviet Union was less rigorous in its demands for obedience, but because its reputation for effective suppression had an intimidating and deterrent effect on those who might wish to rebel. In many Third World nations despotic governments were cruel enough to invite rebellion and not strong enough to make the rebels despair of success. In countries like India, in which a mature leadership is sincerely opposed to domestic violence, a lack of efficiency and control makes possible such tragedies as the 1983 massacres during the election campaign in Assam.

Many Third World leaders have attracted world sympathy by the pathos of their struggle for national independence, but few of them have shown a consuming interest in the dull prose of economic planning. Many of them have preferred the facile satisfactions of international and continental diplomacy.

The colonial guilt argument is no longer effective. The present generation of citizens in the rich countries were born in a noncolonial age and do not feel any culpability for what their forefathers wrought. Present-day Norwegians and Swedes do not suffer from a pressing need to atone for the excesses of the Vikings.

It is common to castigate the wealthy countries for spending so much of their resources on armaments, but the Third World is in the arms business more deeply than would have seemed possible two decades ago. Leaders in the Third World have not even made a convincing effort to show that transfers of wealth would be a transfer to peoples and not only to governments and armies. The world as a whole spends a large percentage of the planetary product on preparation for war. Most of this expenditure is by the superpowers, but the Third World has been spending some one hundred billion dollars a year on arms.

Third World leaders would be on stronger ground if they

abandoned the pretense of moral superiority and took their stand on the notion of a common interest and an increasing interdependence between the richer and poorer nations.

There is a manifest need for both sides to revise the style and tone of their dialogue. The rich countries should realize that they are not dealing with philanthropy but with a vital element of their own stability. The Third World needs to replace confrontation, which has failed, by persuasion, which has not been tried.

Men and women of my generation think back nostalgically to the Marshall Plan which stimulated the recovery of Europe. This was a perfect integration of moral duty with enlightened self-interest. Assisting European recovery could be explained to the idealists as an unselfish sharing of resources, and to the hard-headed realists as an intelligent device for saving threatened societies from Communist domination. Indeed, each of these arguments was effectively deployed by the Truman administration when it asked a parsimonious Congress to make allocations for European recovery.

It is evident that the European example cannot convincingly be applied to other areas of the world. The beneficiaries of the Marshall Plan were established nation-states with similar habits of thought and reaction. The European leaders shared common values and felt themselves to be united under the banner of the *Corpus Christianum*. They were also spurred by the sting of desperate need; all of them understood that another great conflict would exhaust their energies and banish them from history.

The Third World nations do not even have a unifying common factor. They vary from the opulence of Kuwait and Saudi Arabia through the bright promise of Nigeria and Brazil to the desperate poverty of Haiti and Bangladesh.

To grasp the complexity of the situation we must understand that the solution of development problems does not lie exclusively in pumping resources or technologies from the wealthy countries into the hungry ones. Technological modernization is essential to long-term material growth, but not every nation cherishes material growth as the worthiest ambition.

When multinational corporations become the principal carriers of technologies, we face a psychological difficulty. Western technology involves the acceptance of the values that go together with rationality, efficiency, and problem solving. What happens when these values are rejected in favor of ancient truths and mystical ideals? Or when nations determine that material progress can only go hand in hand with rigidly organized systems that negate human rights? Or when the United States, as the major donor of aid, embarks on a sharp reduction of its own programs in a revolt against doctrines of multilateralism?

All of these things are happening now, and this is far from being the golden age of foreign aid programs. Yet, when all is said and done and recorded, the fact that foreign international aid flourished during the Cold War sheds a gracious light on the bleak wastes of our storm-ridden century. Billions of dollars and thousands of skilled personnel have been transferred from richer to poorer countries since World War II. This dimension of international cooperation was virtually unknown in previous ages.

I confess that I got an ovation at the 1963 United Nations Conference on Science and Technology in the Development of New States by asking rhetorically, "What is our aim—to colonize the moon, or to save this planet from the destruction of its resources?" I ceased to be proud of the ovation as soon as I sat down and reflected that the states that spend vast sums on arms and space research are precisely those which sustain the development enterprise across the world.

My conclusion is that anyone who pretends that ethical impulses have dominated diplomatic history would have a very hard time in proving his case. Domestic politics are fundamentally consensual, since all parties in society would suffer from mistaken decisions in peace and war, or in economic policies. Foreign policy, on the other hand, is intrinsically conflictual, since competition and rivalry are built into the separatist mentalities of nation-states.

Mankind has never had, and probably will never have, a unified vision of right, wrong, peace, war, fidelity, betrayal, pride, and glory, but states have often been able to converge toward a common interest based on prudence and reciprocal advantage.

3 The Perils of Analogy

Analogy tells us that if two situations are similar in some respects, they are probably similar in all respects, or at least in most of them. This reasoning is based on a sense of kinship between diplomacy and the legal profession, which is also obsessed by precedents. Lawyers believe that the decisions of learned judges in past ages are radiant with durable truths which are capable of illuminating future choices.

Unfortunately, diplomacy and law are not part of the same intellectual family. The judge asks, "To which of two contending parties should I award the judgment?" The diplomat asks, "How can I give a measure of remedy to each of them?" The theme of a judgment is decision, the theme of a diplomatic process is compromise. A diplomatic negotiation typically ends with neither party ecstatically victorious or abjectly humiliated.

Policymakers who base their conclusions on analogy and experience are on particularly dangerous ground in the transition to the nuclear age. Their experiences are of an era in which many of the present-day sovereignties did not exist, in which European problems dominated international diplomacy, and decisions about peace or war suddenly came to have a gravity unlike anything known before. In this new world, international events, like fingerprints, are marked by particularity, not by similarity. Nothing is less valuable than a nonnuclear metaphor about the nuclear era.

Yet statesmen and diplomats, ignoring the disparities which separate the present condition from the past, persistently think backward to a previous experience. They assume that nations have been in conflict so often and for so long that they are unlikely to find a situation for which there is no precedent in the past. They then seek to apply solutions which once proved effective in the belief that analogous situations are bound to recur.

When I delivered the Lauterpacht lectures at Cambridge University some years ago, I attempted a visual exercise. I brought into the Senate House building a red rubber ball and a shiny red apple, and then described analogy in the following terms: "This apple is round, red, shiny, and good to eat. This rubber ball is round, red, and shiny. Therefore, there is at least a strong probability that it will be good to eat."

The basic truth is that circumstances in which situations differ from each other may precisely be those that define their essential nature. I come back to the statement of the French philosopher Paul Valéry: "History is the science of things which do not repeat themselves." A Harvard biologist, Stephen Jay Gould, has gone even further. He wrote that "our empirical world is a temporal sequence of complex events, so unrepeatable by the laws of probability and so irreversible by principles of thermodynamics, that everything interesting happens only once in its meaningful details." George Kennan asks: "If this is true of the natural sciences, how could it be otherwise in the social and political ones?"[1]

There are cyclical processes in nature, but not in diplomacy. Therefore, history, including diplomatic history, should be based on the meticulous and separate discussion of particular events.

I now seek to analyze the perils of analogy with a few case histories.

I begin in 1956 with what was then the gravest crisis in the Western world—the coordinated invasion of Egypt by British, French, and Israeli forces. The two major imperial powers and Israel were protesting, with legal justification, against the nationalization of the Suez Canal by President Nasser. The British and French governments were eager to restore the Suez Canal to international control. Israel had a totally different and more limited motivation. Its aim was to open the international waterway to free Israeli access and also to slow down the dangerous rate of Egyptian rearmament and to resist fedayeen commando raids.

The fact that the three countries were not pursuing the same objectives was one of the causes of their subsequent disarray.

The most experienced Western statesman of that era was the British prime minister, Anthony Eden. He was in fact probably overexperienced. His mind was dominated by recollections of previous crises in which he had played what was generally regarded as an admirable role. He now wrote to President Eisenhower that there was a close analogy between Nasser's defiance of international law in seizing the Suez Canal and Hitler's conquest of the Rhineland.[2]

Eden returned to this theme on at least seven occasions in a vain attempt to mobilize the United States for the tripartite invasion. The implication was that if Nasser was not thwarted in the attempted seizure of the Suez Canal, we could expect a sequence of aggressions that would bring fearful tragedy on the world. In Eden's view, the nationalization of the canal would come to be regarded as the equivalent to Hitler's conquests of European capitals from Austria, to Czechoslovakia, to Poland, and later Brussels, Amsterdam, and Paris, as well as a great part of Russia.

Eden was talking nonsense. The two situations in which he saw close analogy were different both in proportion and in their essential nature. In proportion, because an action of minor consequence cannot rationally be analogous to events of thunderous and gigantic repercussion. In essential nature, because the seizure of a canal on Egyptian soil by a medium-sized country like Egypt could, as events ultimately proved, be absorbed by the world system without results similar to the horrors inflicted by Hitler on mankind. The Nazi invasion of the Rhineland was the first link in a chain of violence initiated by what was then the strongest military power that had ever existed. It was not "similar" to anything else in world history, and Egypt had no ambition or power to create such a consequence.

Even the legal aspects of Nasser's action were not comparable to Hitler's aggressions. The Suez Canal was under the regime of the Suez Canal Maritime Company that was administered by France and subsidized by Britain, which had seized military control some eighty years previously. The two imperial powers believed, with colonialist certainty, that the uneducated Egyptians would not know how to undertake the acrobatic task of putting ships through the canal. This proved quite untrue. When the test came some years later, Egyptian pilots needed only two weeks to master the art of piloting ships through the canal without mishap.

The military failure of the Suez expedition turned out to be a disaster for Europe. The issue may appear trivial, but its consequences were immense. The failure of the Suez enterprise ended with the two European empires losing their independent strategic roles. From that point on, Britain and France virtually disappeared from the center of international responsibility. The strategic map became bipolar. France and Britain decided—in the French case with speed and success, in the British case with reluctance—to seek a future within a European context. France under Charles de Gaulle's leadership concealed its defeat by an assertive foreign policy, lecturing Americans about the Vietnam War, blocking British entry into the European Community, traveling to Canada to undermine Ottawa's hold on Quebec, and stressing France's independence of American tutelage. But de Gaulle knew as well as anyone that all these actions did not compensate France for the loss of its great power status. British governments, led by Prime Minister Harold Macmillan, began a long, laborious attempt to secure integration into the European Community. Instead of a United Nations dominated by "five permanent members of the Security Council" (Britain, France, the United States, the Soviet Union, and China), there would henceforth be only two dominant powers, the United States and the Soviet Union.

The Suez crisis, to be sure, had coincided with the invasion of Hungary by Soviet forces, but the latter merely confirmed an existing condition. It did not create new alignments, since the Soviet Union's great power status was already in place without challenge.

I personally came to understand this changing pattern of power vividly when I returned to Washington after an abrasive encounter in Paris with President de Gaulle, who had refused to praise the Israeli victory in the recent Arab-Israeli war. President Lyndon Johnson asked me what de Gaulle had said. I replied, "President de Gaulle believes that the four great powers should concert their action." Johnson growled defiantly, "Who the hell are the other two?"

The sentiment that Britain and France were no longer capable of acting independently without American support has characterized their policies up to the present day. When the Gulf War erupted against Iraq in 1990, British and French forces were the only ones which gave substantive support to the American forces, but they did so only after exploring the ground carefully, with the United States, and accepting its command. The Suez-Sinai expedition was the only war ever inspired by and expounded in accordance with a specific analogy from which its main author, Prime Minister Eden, never departed at any time.

It is true that when President Truman ordered American resistance to North Korea in 1950, he thought intensively about the Japanese invasion of Manchuria, which he believed to be one of the prime causes of World War II. But he did not belabor this analogy. Indeed, it is ironic to recall that no leading statesman has ever praised the analogy of another leading statesman. When U.S. Secretary of State John Foster Dulles used the "Rhineland argument" to justify the use of force against the insurgents in Indo-China, Eden primly retorted: "I was not convinced by the assertion which Mr. Dulles then made, that the situation in Indo-China was analogous to the Japanese invasion of Manchuria in 1931 and to Hitler's reoccupation of the Rhineland."[3]

More gravely, the advocates of American intervention in Vietnam from the 1960s onward constantly sought popularity for their decision by comparing it with the Korean War, which had been acceptable to American public opinion. This habit became so rampant that a far-sighted opponent of the Vietnam War, Under Secretary of State George Ball, felt bound to make a patient analysis of the differences which violated the analogy. He pointed out that the Korean intervention, unlike that in Vietnam, had been sustained by the United Nations despite the failure of the absent Soviet Union to cast its veto; that the United States, as a result, had active support from other countries, including fifty-three that contributed troops, whereas in Vietnam the United States had gone it alone. Ball pointed out that South Korea, unlike South Vietnam, had a stable government. The South Koreans were ready to fight for their independence, whereas the South Vietnamese, who had been at war for twenty years, had no such energy or commitment. The Korean War, explained Ball, was a response to a classic land invasion by a hundred thousand troops across a recognized frontier. It therefore gave the United States an unassailable political and legal base for counteraction.[4]

These differences were so self-evident that it is disturbing to think of a high official of a great power needing laborious explanations. Yet at no time did the policymakers concerned with

Vietnam manage to liberate themselves from the Rhineland and Korean analogies.

American policymakers, who were so lucid in rejecting Eden's analogies about Suez, were bewitched by the idea that the Vietnam War was similar to the Allies' war against Hitler. The protagonists of the Vietnam War called themselves "the best and the brightest." They were undoubtedly animated by a genuine sense of international danger. Their reasoning was that if the insurgents in Indo-China were to win, the other countries in that region and beyond would fall, one by one, like a row of dominoes. Laos, Cambodia, Thailand, the Philippines, Burma, and Singapore would collapse, and the plague of collapsing regimes might extend as far as Australia and New Zealand. "Either we make a stand here or we lose the whole of Asia" was a theme that reverberated from the rhetoric of Presidents Eisenhower and Kennedy, and most of all Johnson. Many years were to pass, and fifty-eight thousand American soldiers would lose their lives, before it dawned on American opinion that it was wildly illogical to accept a Communist state in Cuba, less than a hundred miles away, and to fight to the point of exhaustion against the danger of a Communist state establishing itself six thousand miles away in Vietnam!

Hovering over the scene like an ominous cloud was the shadow of Munich. There is no doubt that Robert McNamara, McGeorge Bundy, and the Pentagon chiefs were inspired by the Munich syndrome—the conviction that unless aggression was checked everywhere, no part of the world would be safe anywhere. This doctrine of universal American responsibility had first been enunciated by President Kennedy, who brought his country closer to the brink of nuclear war than any other President before or after. In his memorably eloquent inaugural address he had said: "We shall pay any price, bear any burden, meet any hardship, support any friend, oppose any foe, to ensure the survival and success of liberty."[5]

This was an analogy-ridden idea: Almost all international conflicts were conceived as a gigantic analogy under the heading of the "survival and success of liberty." "The best and the brightest" were dominated by an activist spirit reflecting their generation's experience in World War II. They were determined not to be caught unprepared again. They were unsentimental and not afflicted by self-doubt. Not even the fiasco of the Bay of Pigs adventure had caused them to modify their credulity about the capacity of the United States to police the world.

Under their leadership American policy was dominated by parallel analogies originating from Munich and Vietnam. The major weakness of analogies is that they liberate statesmen from the need to think freshly about particular cases. The argument ran as follows:

> Munich was an attempt to solve a crisis by a negotiated compromise.
> Munich was a disastrous failure.
> Therefore, any attempt to solve a crisis by a negotiated compromise should be avoided.
>
> Vietnam was an attempt to solve a problem by military resistance.
> Vietnam was a failure.
> Therefore, any attempt to solve a problem by military resistance should be avoided.

If compromise and resistance are both excluded from the repertoire of diplomacy, there is precious little left. The idea that each crisis must be approached through independent exploration and analysis would not become a United States habit for many years. After the Cold War, when the Soviet Union no longer obsessed the political thinking of the United States, the idea of selectivity began to take hold. It became accepted doctrine that the United States had an interest in defending oil-rich Kuwait without being automatically involved in defending Bosnia. One scholar objected: "Our government is investigating individual phenomena, treating events as if each of them were unique, instead of searching out among them the uniformities and the parallels required for generalization."

Note the phrase "as if each of them were unique." That is the crux. Surely all the evidence indicates that each international situation really *is* unique. Each is influenced by human fallibility. All international problems cannot be solved by rigorous formulas. A system that makes no allowance for contingency, emotion, and personality is unlikely to lead to better solutions than the imperfect classical method of individual analysis.

Many celebrated historians went to their honored graves believing that most phenomena, including the rise and fall of empires, are much like other, similar events.

An interesting dissident expounding an opposite view has gone unnoticed. He did not write in a "fashionable" language. He was the greatest of Arab historians, Ibn Khaldun, who lived in Tunisia in the fourteenth century. In his *Introduction to History* he wrote:

> Scholars are of all people those least fitted for politics and its ways. The reason for this is that they are accustomed to intellectual speculation, the search for concepts, and the abstraction from sense data and clarification in the mind. All their operations aim at attaining the universal aspect of things, not those particular to their material content, or to a person, generation, nation, or particular class of men. . . . *In fact, no social phenomenon should be judged by analogy with other phenomena, for if it is similar to them in certain respects it may yet differ from them in many others.* . . . The ordinary sound man of mediocre intelligence, whose mind is unaccustomed to such speculation, judges each case on its own merits.[6]

If Ibn Khaldun considered mediocrity to be the best qualifica-tion for statecraft, it is unfortunate that he is not alive today to draw consolation from the contemporary international scene.

A very recent writer summarizes the analogy principle by placing its full burden on a single statesman.

> The president emerges as a leader imprisoned by historical analogies—the New Deal showing the wonderful curative powers of governmental intervention on behalf of eco-nomic development, Munich demonstrating the folly of negotiating with aggressors, Korea the dangers of uncon-trollable escalation, and the Cuban missile crisis the virtues of using American power in a tough but calibrated fashion. Add all this up—as Johnson, the consummate consensus politician was ever ready to do—and the all-out limited war to defeat aggression seems utterly inevitable and massively overdetermined.[7]

Most governments and foreign ministries use the assistance of academic experts who continually search for unifying explana-tions. Few universities have working diplomats on their faculties. Ideal or fanciful notions about how the diplomatic process works echo across many campuses on the basis of theoretical models. It is hard to imagine a professor of surgery who has never per-formed a single operation, but there are many professors of inter-national relations who have never negotiated an agreement or argued a case in the international forum.

The fiasco at Munich does not invalidate all negotiated com-promises. The failure of the Vietnam War does not eliminate the need for armed resistance to aggression in better circumstances. Anthony Eden's breakdown over Suez does not refute the fact that he was right to advocate stern measures against Mussolini and Hitler in the 1930s. The entry of American forces into Gre-nada in 1983 is something that the world could have done with-out, but it is not "equivalent" to the Soviet suppression of Czech independence in 1968, as some opponents of the intervention absurdly declared.

I see no role for analogy except its exclusion from serious diplomatic historiography. Some American historians have got it right: "History smiles at all attempts to force its flow into theoretical patterns or logical grooves: it plays havoc with our generalizations, breaks all our rules. History is baroque."[8]

4 Human Rights Seldom Win

Article 2(7) of the United Nations Charter proclaims with un-usual emphasis: "Nothing contained in the present Charter shall authorize the United Nations to intervene in matters which are essentially within the domestic jurisdiction of any state or shall require the Members to submit such matters to settlement under the present Charter."[1]

So far, well and good. Three cheers for domestic jurisdiction. But article 1(3) of the same Charter also states that one of the manifold "Purposes of the United Nations" is: "To achieve inter-national cooperation in solving international problems of an economic, social, cultural, or humanitarian character, and in pro-moting and encouraging respect for human rights and for funda-mental freedoms for all."[2]

It does not require an exceptional gift of language to deduce that the framers of the UN Charter attached more importance to sovereignty than to the promotion of human rights. But the end result is that one provision of the Charter invites active interven-tion in human rights issues, while a stronger injunction says, "Please keep your distinguished noses out of such concerns."

There were good pragmatic reasons for the priority given to sovereignty. The international system is composed of sovereign states and is not greatly inspired by the ideal of world community. In these conditions, disrespect for sovereignty would expose the international system to anarchy. Every nation knows exactly what is wrong with the human rights record of all other nations, and it is hard to think of a single state that would have signed a UN Charter which did not contain an article defending domestic jurisdiction. On the other hand, some governments would have accepted the absence of an allusion to human rights in the United Nations Charter with docility and resignation. There had been no mention of human rights in the League of Nations Covenant.

Yet, on deeper reflection, the savage outrage committed against civilian populations in World War II would have been callously ignored if the UN had followed the League of Nations in refusing to mention human rights among other "problems of an economic, social, cultural, or humanitarian character."

This sharp conflict between two beneficent ideals goes far to prove that great virtues are not necessarily compatible. This disconcerting truth runs through all domains of human action and thought. Courage is not always compatible with prudence, liberty with equality, moral piety with realism, intellectual rigor with the free flow of imagination. Freedom for the wolves can spell catastrophe for the lambs.

In international relations, the conflict between desirable ends is especially sharp, since diplomacy and ethics operate on the basis of discordant premises. Ethics postulate absolute values, while diplomatic solutions are by their nature ambiguous. A diplomatic solution is one in which neither party attains all its objectives, while neither suffers the humiliation of total defeat. That is why diplomatic solutions rarely become clarion calls to audacity, sacrifice, martyrdom, and heroic suicide of the kind that make an indelible mark on history. Faced by a conflict between two values each charged with virtue, the diplomat cannot escape the necessity of choice. He usually ends up with a sliding scale in which both virtues are given no more than partial effect. In diplomacy you cannot have everything. This contrasts, of course, with the sure clarity of Abraham Lincoln when he said that "in great contests both sides claim to be acting in the name of God. Both may be wrong and one must be wrong. God cannot be on both sides at the same time."

I have never been impressed by the perceived division of American statesmen between the "idealist" and the "realist" schools. Most realists pay sincere devotion to ethical values and most of the idealists acknowledge the overriding claims of national interest.

No two conflicting ideas are more difficult to reconcile than the promotion of universal human rights and respect for sovereignty. The former value incites the kind of intervention which the latter sternly forbids.

Although few people confess to apathy about the importance of human rights, the active and purposeful implementation of humanitarian policies has proved complex. The question is, what happens when the promotion of human rights collides with what seem more urgent or more attainable objectives? Arthur Schlesinger, Jr., constructed a depressing but starkly realistic balance sheet about the Carter administration:

> Diplomats objected when the human rights campaign threatened arms control negotiations or political relationships. . . . Businessmen objected when the campaign hurt exports. Carter himself, the presumed number one human rights crusader, was soon found visiting authoritarian nations, selling them arms and saluting their leaders. His human rights policy, it appeared, was compatible with effusive support for the Shah of Iran, [and] with an egregious letter of commendation to Somosa in Nicaragua. . . . Washington was fearless in denouncing abuses in countries like

Cambodia, Paraguay and Uganda, where the United States had negligible strategic and economic interests; a good deal less fearless toward South Korea, Saudi Arabia, Yugoslavia and most of black Africa; circumspect about the Soviet Union; totally silent about China.[3]

Selectivity in criticism of the Soviet Union for its violation of human rights easily won support from both the liberal and the hawkish wings of President Carter's own party, but it cannot be said to have improved the basis for arms control negotiations, on which Carter understandably placed a higher value. The reduction of the danger of nuclear war by arms control agreements was both crucial and attainable, whereas the hope of moderating the Soviet Union's domestic repressions seemed dubious. Why not pursue the aim which is in real prospect rather than a quixotic hope that has little chance of fulfillment?

The defense of human rights often undercuts more urgent policy goals. In Brazil the U.S. administration's denunciations of human rights violations created the wrong atmosphere for persuading Brazilians to reverse their nuclear agreement with West Germany. Argentina, under the rule of the brutal generals, was frequently and ineffectively chastised by the White House but found little reason to respect the Carter administration's trade embargo on the Soviet Union in January 1980.

Not only was American human rights policy often accused of inconsistency, it was also tainted by what looked like insincerity. In Iran, for example, Carter praised the shah lavishly in a December 1977 toast, describing Iran as "an island of stability." In his memoirs, *Keeping Faith,* Carter defends his policy of emphasizing human rights in the American dialogue with foreign states, but he evades the issue of selectivity; his effusive toast to the shah is discreetly omitted from his writings. Yet, unlike all his predecessors, Carter did introduce human rights as an effective theme in international politics. It is true that he ran up against the realities of life in the international struggle between nation-states, jealous of their jurisdictions, and human rights activists on the look-out for injustices and cruelties. Carter forced many countries into defensive postures and gave heart to dissidents and victims of persecution who would have been depressed by an atmosphere of international silence. No American leader since Woodrow Wilson was more insistent than Jimmy Carter on placing human rights squarely on the international agenda.

The question of human rights played a large part in the détente dialogue, especially after the Helsinki Conference, at which the Soviet Union secured recognition of its territorial gains in Eastern Europe. The West seemed to have no real sanction with which to retaliate against Soviet violation of the Helsinki agreement on human rights. It was quite an achievement to get a Soviet signature on the human rights provision of Basket 1 and Basket 3 of the Helsinki Final Act. To get the Soviets actually to honor this signature would have been a double victory. It would in fact have been too good to believe.

One of the many paradoxes in this story was the hesitation of liberal intellectuals to protest against the persecution of Jews in the Soviet Union for their links with Israel. This policy was particularly inept because the Soviet statesman Andrei Gromyko, in his April 1947 speech at the United Nations, had supported the Zionist idea, including a reference to the historic roots that bind Jews to Israel. Some American intellectuals recoiled from criticizing the Soviet authorities on the grounds that it was more important to preserve international conciliation than to dream of liberalizing the Soviet system.

A typical reaction came from the American sociologist David Riesman:

> I am in a position of deep moral ambiguity because, on the one hand, I admire enormously the courage of the Soviet dissidents . . . but at the same time I have consistently re-

fused to sign petitions or in any other way to lend my name
to criticisms of the treatment of these dissidents. In a bipolar nuclear world we cannot afford to hold to a simple,
straightforward universalist moral standard such as one
might hope for in a world free from the threat of mass annihilation. . . . It is because I see the nuclear question as always foremost that I cannot be sanguine about human
prospects in the long run, unless the human rights issue of
the moment in [America] is made less salient.[4]

In similar terms George Kennan, after expressing sincere support for the dissidents and declaring sensitive devotion to individual rights, went on to declare that he saw no point in "constant
incantations" about the violation of fundamental freedoms in the
Soviet Union. The implication was that he believed criticism to
be likely to irritate the USSR and to interfere with the larger
objective of securing agreements with the Soviet Union on arms
control.

Many liberals did put peace ahead of human rights as a moral
imperative and refused to badger the Soviet Union into reforms
which the Soviet view of society could not accommodate. On
the other hand, the American hawks had no compunction in
assailing human rights violations by Communist regimes while
casting indulgent eyes on the transgressions of Iran (under the
shah's regime), Cambodia, Turkey, Chile, and the Philippines.

The notion that there was an inherent conflict between a campaign for human rights and the promotion of East-West agreements in pursuit of world peace had paradoxical results. When
the intellectuals or liberals were silent or lenient about Soviet
persecution of dissidents, they left the human rights field open to
the opponents of détente. The Soviets then developed the theme
that the vocal defenders of human rights were more concerned
with pursuing the Cold War than with helping dissidents in the
USSR. This was unfair; it was objectively possible to be against

the escalation of the arms race and also to condemn Soviet treatment of Jews and other minorities.

I never believed that the Soviet position on East-West relations
would be negatively affected by pressure in Western countries on
behalf of a better Soviet record in human rights. The USSR was
always guided in strategic matters by a cold appraisal of its own
interests and anxieties. Yet with all its ostensible imperviousness
to external pressure, the Soviet Union maintained a high degree
of sensitivity to world opinion, especially to that part of it which
the Soviets defined as "progressive" or "peace-loving."

Kennan may have underestimated the positive effects of "incantations" against human rights violations. They might be self-
evident and repetitive for those who proclaim them, but they are
essential if we wish the dissidents to retain their capacity of resistance. The absence of "incantations" could only demoralize
those in the Soviet Union who had striven to moderate the
severity of Soviet policies within the limits of feasibility. Western
silence could easily have become a form of intervention on behalf
of tyrannical procedures in Third World countries. There was
also the corrosive effect on the democratic cause of an unwilling-
ness by democrats to celebrate their own values in loud and clear
tones. Communist ideology never seemed to suffer from such
inhibitions.

Those who refrained from uttering their criticism of human
rights abuses in the Soviet Union, in South Africa, and in many
dictatorships should have had one important consideration in
mind: Nothing is more terrible in a prison where men and
women are tortured for their beliefs than the silence of civilized
communities.

One of the more incisive justifications for the silence of liberal
writers and thinkers was the conviction that the persecuting governments were unlikely to change their conduct and might even
aggravate their severities. This was certainly true of the Nazis in
the heyday of their atrocities, but it was a rule with significant

exceptions. One of them was South Africa, where the downfall of apartheid was demonstrably influenced by world opinion as expressed in the United Nations and by individual governments. To a lesser degree, the tendency of the Soviet authorities to mitigate their oppression came to expression before glasnost and perestroika.

I had personal experience of this trend. After breaking relations with Israel in 1967, the Soviet Union entered a long period of abstention from contact. In December 1973, contact was resumed when Foreign Minister Gromyko received me for a significant talk in Geneva, where the first Arab-Israeli peace conference was held. When I raised the question of the treatment of Jews and the ridiculous policy of persecuting the Hebrew language (as if a language can be guilty of anything that is written in it), Gromyko exploded in wrath. He said: "Whenever a foreign minister comes to see me, instead of discussing his relationship with us, he starts talking abut the Jews and Israel. Why do you incite against the Soviet Union?" In that context he mentioned Canada, France, and all the Scandinavian countries.

Some of my colleagues in Jerusalem were disconcerted by this irascibility, since we were deeply interested in a rapprochement with Moscow. I saw Gromyko's rage as a good omen. If the Soviets really believed that their attitude toward Israel and the Jewish dissidents was a hindrance to their international relations, there was a better chance that they would move to moderate it. They did in fact increase the number of Jews to whom they accorded the right of emigration, partly in an effort to qualify for concessions by the United States in the economic field, but also with the Jewish question in mind.

As I listened tensely to Gromyko's tirade, my mind went back to a previous encounter with one of his predecessors, Andrei Vyshinski. In 1953 I was elected to one of the vice presidencies of the General Assembly of the United Nations. This is a post with invisible duties, but it did cause me to be invited to UN parties at which protocol seated me next to Vyshinski, with whom anyone would dislike being stranded on a desert island. On one such occasion, inspired by the conviction that I would have nothing to lose, I said: "Andrei Andreyevitch, why don't you let the Jews go? You would lose nothing and might gain something important." His reply may have been influenced by a prodigious, prior intake of vodka: "What do you mean by saying that we would lose nothing? If we let the Jews leave, everyone would want to leave."

The next morning he telephoned my UN embassy in a tense mood. "What I said last night was joke. Was—how you call it—humor? Since was joke I assume you did not find necessary to send telegram?" I reassured him about "telegram" since I had already sent a written account to Jerusalem, although not in telegram form. He had evidently seen ahead of him a future to be spent in Siberia.

It could be said that in the cases of South Africa and the Soviet Union, world opinion was not the only factor in the relaxation of suppressive measures. There were also sanctions. In the South African case these were based on international judgments, whereas in the Soviet Union the United States could either grant or withhold "most favored nation" status. These conspicuous instances argue powerfully against the notion that pressure on totalitarian countries to relax their cruelties is invariably a lost cause.

However, 1995 ended with two instances that held contrary evidence. They concerned China and Saudi Arabia.

China had received high-level visits by American representatives. Beijing had offered nothing in return. It had maintained a horrific level of suppression, an unprecedented rate of penal executions and detentions, without trial or due process, and had conducted ominous military exercises near the coast of Taiwan. Its brutalities reached a climax with the shooting of students and dissidents in Tienanmen Square under the glare of television cameras. Later came reports of mass executions in China for felonies which would not have qualified for such punishments in

civilized countries. Visits to China by leading American statesmen had no alleviating effect. The United States permitted a
huge international conference on women's rights to be convened
by the United Nations in Beijing at a time when the attitude of
Chinese authorities to women's rights was beneath acceptable
standards. The persecution by China of Tibetan nationalists was
ferocious, and for many anxious weeks the Chinese military
forces were carrying out provocative maneuvers that seemed to
threaten Taiwan.

An American mission to China in 1996 concluded that "issues
relating to Taiwan's future have reemerged as the most dangerous
possible causes of military conflict in East Asia." The report argued that private, "non-official efforts by American and international organizations are generally more effective in correcting human rights abuses than highly visible U.S. government actions."[5]

The only effective weapon in the hands of the United States
would have been the denial of most favored nation status to
China.

The Chinese market had a seductive appeal for American trading partners. Not many years would elapse before it would sur-
pass the markets of the United States and of an enlarged European Union, but in the short run China would have more to lose
than to gain from restrictive American measures directed against
the Chinese economy. China was more likely to resent American
pressure and to refuse to adopt U.S. humanitarian standards than
to bow to American wishes on human rights.

The Clinton administration, which had risked the lives of
American soldiers in Somalia, Bosnia, and Haiti in an effort to
improve the lot of oppressed populations, had second and third
thoughts when it came to discussing the withholding of trade
relations with China. After much deliberative torment a clear
decision was taken. The United States virtually ruled that trade
with the potentially vast Chinese market had a higher priority
than the exercise of pressure on China to change its human rights

policies. It decided that free commerce with what eventually would become the world's largest market must take precedence over exacerbating American-Chinese relations by punitive measures of any serious kind. President Clinton decided to offer most favored nation trading privileges to China.

The American mission reported further that "a focus on a few high-profile cases of dissidents may not always help them and may actually weaken the cause of long-term political reform." The severity of this judgment may be better understood when we realize that the fate of individual dissidents had done more to stir public indignation against Beijing's lamentable human rights record than anything else.

There is high drama in the confrontation between the United States and China on the issue of human rights, and no agreed solution is yet in sight. The contending parties are the only superpower and the most populous country in the world, with the potentially largest market.

The current situation is almost intolerable for both parties. To maintain the status quo, the United States would have to renounce its cherished reputation as the vigilant guardian of human rights in the world. This would mean the amputation of one of the main principles of American policy and rhetoric. It is hard to imagine the United States being able to continue the litany of excuses by which it offers cover for an increasingly harsh human rights record in China. It is in the nature of suppressive regimes to escalate in severity, not to modify their practices. On the Chinese side, the dependence on cheap labor and a notoriously savage system of penalties for dissidence is bound to result in a succession of explosive incidents which would produce a crescendo of indignant reactions leading to something like the anti-apartheid agitation in South Africa.

The slightest reaction of that sort would compel the United States to be true to its own tradition and to absorb the resultant Chinese rage. The addition of Hong Kong, Taiwan, and Tibet to the list of American acrimonies will soon make confrontation so inevitable that most friends of America would probably advise that any change will have to come from the Chinese side.

A contemporary incident in the United Kingdom sent a similar message in a more intimate, individual context. A Saudi dissident resident in Britain had been agitating peacefully but incisively against what he called violations of human rights in that kingdom. The Saudis exercised pressure on Britain to end these activities. The plea became a threat; at issue were Saudi purchases of weapons and equipment from Britain to the flabbergasting amount of three billion dollars. The Saudi authorities assumed that this windfall was more relevant to Britain's economic future than the liberty of Mohammed Masrawi to continue his alleged "provocations."

The British government did not plan to return the "culprit" to his own kingdom, where the methods of treating dissidents are notoriously abrasive. London sought a more congenial asylum on the island of Dominica. It was unlikely that Dominica would offer a propaganda platform as effective as London, but Britain had no obligation to secure particular resonance for anti-Saudi propaganda.

It might seem that two nations with a record of concern for human rights have simply abandoned the human rights arena. It is difficult to condone, but not hard to understand, their motives. President Clinton was not elected for the purpose of reforming the system of justice in China or upholding the rights of Taiwanese and Tibetans. He was specifically mandated by his electorate to further the interests of Americans in the expansion of their economic welfare. Prime Minister John Major was not charged by British voters with the task of mitigating the ferocious rigors of the Saudi penal system. His allotted task was to seek as much advantage as possible from the high quality of British technology.

The question is whether and at which point the violation of a human right becomes so outrageous that the excuse of domestic jurisdiction loses validity. This point was clearly reached and exceeded by the savagery of the Nazi regime against the Jews and other Holocaust victims, by Stalin's purges, and by the butchery of the Rwandans. In the two specific cases I have discussed here, only a pedantically principled government would have thought that the maintenance of Mr. Masrawi in his London activity was worth the loss of three billion dollars to the country that sheltered him.

As for the United States and China, there may be some reason to hope that an America in a reciprocal relationship with China may one day infect that country with the better American tradition on human rights. This, in fact, is one of the justifications invoked by the governments which take a pragmatic rather than a self-righteous view of human rights violations. They do not believe that punitive measures are effective, while free trading practices may in time create common interests and values.

Punitive measures are certainly least effective in countries where cruel practices are linked to religious convictions. Fundamentalist interpretations of Islam, often based on Koranic texts, are immune to external criticism. In Iran under the rule of Ayatollah Khomeini and his successors, the summary execution of offenders against the legal system and their submission to flagellation are defended by governments on grounds of religious freedom. Since the free exercise of religious liberty is a principle zealously protected by international law, judicial savagery faces Western governments with serious dilemmas. How can one overcome measures which are inadmissible in Western eyes but fully sanctioned by the piety and faith of those who uphold them?

Despite a loudly trumpeted UN conference held, incongruously, in Beijing, very few religions are egalitarian in their attitude to women's rights. Most lay claim to exclusive revelation. In Saudi Arabia, activities of the kind that are not subject to judicial penalties in most countries, such as drinking alcoholic beverages, are punished by severe whipping, and persistent offenders against the dictates of faith or law can face decapitation.

Islamic fundamentalism is not on the decline. In the fall of 1996 its tenets were upheld by the Taliban movement in Afghanistan. Afghan women suddenly found themselves barred from any except household functions and many schools and universities had to close their doors. Islamic fundamentalism has become a metaphor for internecine violence and hate.

Islamic fundamentalist societies do not respect existing law in their own lands. In the Middle East conflict, Palestinian dissident organizations, such as Hamas and Hizbollah, do not even obey the enactments of the nationalist leaders who led them to self-government under the banner of the Palestine Liberation Organization. Internal disturbances thus degenerate into something like civil war. In Israel, Jewish settlers in territories of disputed allegiance have allowed themselves to ignore the edicts of cabinets and parliaments and have refused to obey the laws restraining violence.

On November 4, 1995, an Orthodox Jewish zealot assassinated Prime Minister Yitzhak Rabin in a public square. Before that tragedy, the opponents of the peace process, including the Likud party leaders, had organized virulent demonstrations against Rabin, which the bereaved family believe contributed to the crime.

It would be possible to draw a more favorable judgment about human rights in Israel if there were no statues and mausoleums extolling such men as Dr. Baruch Goldstein, who massacred twenty-nine guiltless Muslims in Hebron while they were helplessly prostrate in prayer, resigning themselves, as the Islamic faith dictates, to what they saw as a superhuman divinity.

Prime Minister Rabin had led great armies in war and had greatly enhanced his nation's security, whereas his assassin, now languishing in jail, "contributed" nothing but blood, hatred, and violence to the Israeli national cause.

On the positive side of the ledger, there is now an impressive UN network of institutions dealing with human rights problems.

These suffer from the very difficulties that the United Nations itself confronts, such as the absence of supranational authority and the difficulty, experienced until the end of the Cold War, in overcoming the divisiveness of UN debates. Neither the stern injunction against encroaching on "domestic jurisdiction" nor the vagueness of the UN Charter's allusions to human rights has prevented the UN or humanitarian organs from discussing human rights issues, or from acting sternly and, sometimes, effectively against persistent violations.

By and large, human rights activity in the UN, humanitarian organizations, and the European Union has been more intense than the cautious language of the UN Charter once seemed to promise.

Organizations that keep a vigilant eye on abuses of human rights, such as Amnesty International, are by their very nature less inhibited than governments, which necessarily pursue a plurality of goals. There is nothing wrong in making the most of their witness, which usually rests on meticulous research.

Leaders who encourage or tolerate torture and other violations of human rights often shrug their shoulders and say, "My conscience is clean." The answer they should receive is that everything stays clean if one does not use it very often.

There is not much that one state can do to change the policies of another, and there is no escape from selectivity in the choice of arenas. But the fact that it is not possible to improve human rights observance everywhere is no reason for not attempting to do so somewhere. World opinion does not command the field, but it is far less impotent than in all previous ages.

5 The Intrusive Media

Diplomacy, which used to be a reserved domain, controlled by specialized elites, is now a public spectacle, open to the winds of change. Nothing has done more to revolutionize the diplomatic craft than the current vogue of persistent media attention.

Any discussion of this change must begin with its most far-reaching aspect: the collapse of reticence and privacy in negotiation. The entry of the media into every level of the negotiating process changes the nature of diplomacy. The modern negotiator cannot escape the duality of his role. He must transact business simultaneously with his negotiating partner and his own public opinion. This requires a total modification of techniques. Whether this is a favorable development or not is irrelevant. It is certainly irreversible. There is no way of putting the clock back to an era in which negotiations were sheltered from domestic constituencies.

Modern statesmen face three problems relating to war: to prevent its eruption, to limit its range and duration—and to end it in conditions likely to prevent its renewal. Diplomacy failed all three of these tests in the wars of 1914–1918 and 1939–1945.

Leaders of nations cannot complain if public opinion now insists on a more vigilant role in the new and terrifying contingencies of the nuclear era.

The conversion of international negotiation from a reserved pursuit into a public spectacle has been particularly intense in this century. The biblical text for open diplomacy was formulated by President Wilson in the first of his Fourteen Points enacted in the Treaty of Versailles in 1919: "Open covenants of peace, openly arrived at, after which there shall be no private international understandings of any kind, but diplomacy shall proceed always frankly and in the public view."[1]

There is a startling extremism in this famous formulation. Openness is celebrated as both a means and an end. The insistence on "no private international understandings of any kind" is a principle that is impossible to fulfill.

Wilson was reacting virtuously against the conspiratorial tradition in which a few major powers used to decide the future of smaller nations without their knowledge, let alone their consent. His dictum had a brief rhetorical triumph but no operative result. Having proclaimed his fidelity to "open covenants," Wilson joined with the leaders of Britain, France, and Italy—David Lloyd George, Georges Clemenceau, and Vittorio Emmanuele Orlando—in a conference more secretive and less respectful of the interests of nonparticipants than any conclave in previous history.

Soon after his explosive defense of open covenants, Wilson attempted a tactical retreat. In a meeting with the U.S. Senate he declared: "When I pronounced for open diplomacy I meant not that there should be no private discussion of delicate matters, but that no secret agreement of any sort should be entered into and that all international relations, *when fixed,* should be open, aboveboard, and explicit."[2]

This was a major revision of doctrine.[3] Unfortunately, the explosive notion of total openness had sent its repercussions into modern thought with such power that Wilson's retreat had little effect. The idea that open debate in large assemblies is more honorable and efficacious than secret diplomacy has never died.

Traditionally, one used to negotiate an agreement with an adversary in conditions of reticence until a draft agreement was reached. At that stage it would have to be submitted for acceptance or rejection by the parties. Today, the media will not agree to be excluded at any stage.

Since it is conventionally—and fallaciously—believed that fair solutions usually lie midway between the positions of contending parties, negotiators are compelled to invent fictitiously excessive demands in order that their real positions should appear moderate. The hard test comes when concessions have to be made. To your negotiating partner, you describe your concession as so painful as to be almost beyond your own endurance. Simultaneously, you whisper to your suspicious constituency that your concession is inherently trivial, and only your own virtuosity and your adversary's gullibility have given it some importance. The trouble is that the wind carries your words in both directions. Your adversary and your constituency each hears what you say to the other.

It is too easy for the moralist to say that this merely proves the intrinsic duplicity of the diplomatic process. A measure of ambivalence on the part of a mediator is inherent in any quest for agreement between parties who really have divergent interests. There is nothing disreputable in emphasizing to each party the specific advantages that each of them would obtain. The difficulty would be reduced if parliamentary leaders and journalists could be convinced that negotiation is not a zero-sum game. It does not follow that what you give to your adversary is necessarily a loss for yourself. That a concession can be useful on balance both to oneself and to one's rival is a truth that responds to the dialectic of real life, but not to the passionate context of international conflict.

The desire of negotiators to begin with secret exploration is not frivolous. Negotiation consists of stages and a result. If a nation hears of concessions offered by its own representatives without also knowing of the corresponding concessions offered by the other side, indignation will explode at the wrong time and the agreement will be lost.

Nobody can reasonably challenge the need to present agreements to public scrutiny before they are put into force. It is quite another thing, however, when negotiators have to present to their constituencies every tactical phase, every trial balloon or tentative proposal, including those submitted for the purpose of stimulating a bargaining climate. It can be demonstrated that international agreements have been endangered through premature exposure to domestic scrutiny.

A former secretary general of the United Nations, Dag Hammarskjöld, who might have been expected by reason of his office to be the high priest of open diplomacy, was totally disillusioned by the modern obsession with public debate. He wrote: "The best results of negotiation cannot be achieved in international life any more than in our private world in the full glare of publicity, with current debate of all moves, unavoidable misunderstandings, inescapable freezing of positions due to considerations of prestige and the temptation to utilize public opinion as an element integrated into the negotiation itself."

This argument, like most sane counsels, was ignored, but Hammarskjöld persisted in his quest for secret negotiation and scored some successes with his "behind-the-scenes" technique. Hammarskjöld saw no reason for the existence of scenes except for the possibility of operating secretly behind them.

The insistence of the media on knowing every stage of a negotiation has become more aggressive in recent years as a result of events in the United States. The American media, after all, have celebrated great triumphs of exposure in the issues of Watergate and Vietnam. These experiences have strengthened the assumption that secrecy is intrinsically sinful while publicity is inherently virtuous. The effect has been to create a fallacious identity between privacy and conspiracy. It is assumed that anything honorable should be capable of immediate exposure to the public view and, conversely, that anything kept in even temporary discretion must be unscrupulous.

Nobody who has been involved in the quest for international peace can accept so sweeping a generalization. As a general rule, revelation has a better sound than secrecy. But if the journalist has the better of the argument about the means, the diplomat sometimes can reply that peace is a higher social and human value than the satisfaction of curiosity. Thus, diplomacy often, though not invariably, wins the argument against the journalist in terms of ultimate ends. The diplomat and the journalist are each acting within the guiding principle of his vocation, but the diplomat striving to avoid war is sometimes on a higher moral plane than the journalist striving to avoid secrecy. The right to know is not always morally superior to the right to peace.

Most people will decide their attitude according to their perception of mass opinion. Is the public wise or foolish? Virtuous or imprudent? Those who advocate uninhibited press coverage generally believe that peoples are well informed and pure of heart, whereas leaders are fallible, vain, corrupt, power-greedy, and insensitive to humane impulses. The argument about diplomatic method becomes an argument about public virtue.

The exaltation of popular wisdom was a common theme of Enlightenment thinking and is sustained by many progressive ideologies. By contrast, the critics of open diplomacy are not prepared to idealize mass opinion. They know that public emotions are not always kindly or prudent. They are often savage and reckless.

Between the two world wars, nobody did more than Walter Lippmann to dethrone public opinion from the deference which it traditionally evoked. He managed to combine a reputation for liberalism with a scorchingly severe contempt of the public mind. His theme was simple: the choices faced by a democracy can only be grasped by people of mature judgment and specialized knowledge. "Public opinion . . . [has] compelled the governments, which usually knew what would have been wiser, or was necessary, or was more expedient, to be too late with too little, or too long with too much, too pacifist in peace and too bellicose in war, too neutralist or appeasing in negotiation or too intransigent. Mass opinion has acquired a mounting power in this century. It has shown itself to be a dangerous master of decisions when the stakes are life and death."[4]

Experience does not confirm Lippmann's view that public opinion invariably works in favor of bellicosity. He himself became the enemy of bellicosity when the Vietnam War escalated during the Johnson administration. Public opinion often stimulates an instinct for resigned passivity. During the 1930s, the fear of retribution from an allegedly pacifist public opinion caused the British government to abstain from the rearmament that might have prevented World War II. The forces represented by the British Labor party stood simultaneously for resistance to Hitler and opposition to British military reinforcement! A few hundred more aircraft in the arsenals of the democracies might have deterred Nazi expansion.

In the late 1960s, American public opinion exercised pressure on the United States negotiators against persistence in the Vietnam War. Henry Kissinger has recorded that the Nixon administration's bargaining position was weakened by evidence that public opinion would settle for unconditional withdrawal without making any demands on Hanoi for reciprocal concessions. Once your fall-back positions are published, you have already fallen back to them.

The case histories are ambiguous. In 1956, Britain's Suez expedition was thwarted by evidence that public opinion was against the war. On the other hand, when Argentina seized the Falkland Islands in April 1982, British public opinion almost compelled the government to strike a pose of extreme rigor and to undertake an extensive and hazardous naval expedition. Left to themselves, the governing elite might well have renounced the islands in view of their blatant marginality. But in that case, Argentina would have continued to be saddled with a horrendously brutal military regime.

A surge of public opinion in democratic countries has insisted on intervening in the debate about nuclear weaponry. On the one hand, it can be said that in an issue so dependent on technical and general understanding it would be wrong to be influenced by emotions or by the scanty knowledge made available by occasional television debates. On the other hand, the pathos and tragedy inherent in the nuclear weapons dilemma strike at the very heart of the human condition. How then can this issue be left to a small group of experts and specialists? An expert has been correctly defined as someone who understands everything, but nothing else.

After the 1967 war in which Israel prevailed over Egypt, it was regarded as a national sin in Middle East public opinion for any Arab minister or high official to meet with Israeli representatives. It was an Israeli interest to indulge this pretense and accept clandestine procedures since the prize—a peace treaty with an Arab state—was a cherished Israeli aim. In this unpromising atmosphere I, as foreign minister, began a dialogue with King Hussein of Jordan. We would usually meet in London, and sometimes in boats in the vicinity of the ports at Aqaba and Eilat. If these encounters had been reported, our Jordanian partner would have been seriously compromised and the dialogue, which laid foundations for an eventual peace treaty, would probably have been abruptly ended. The same is true of a meeting in Morocco in 1977 between Moshe Dayan, then foreign minister of Israel, and a high Egyptian diplomat. This encounter paved the way for a public negotiation which led to a peace treaty between Israel and Egypt in 1979.

Public opinion often inhibits the slow ripening of wisdom. Most American statesmen were convinced by the end of the 1960s that the United States should correct its relations with China. But the effort was delayed for several years because successive administrations had created a circular dilemma. First, they had nourished a fierce hostility to China, which they had imposed on a public opinion traditionally friendly to the Chinese people. Subsequently, when American leaders were ready to change their position, they feared that the public would not welcome a change of course. They thus subordinated themselves to the demonization of China which they had propagated across many years. They erred twice—once in creating the prejudice, and once in underestimating their own capacity to eradicate it. They would have suffered no great damage in public opinion by making the opening to China at an earlier date.

The difficulties the United States encountered in adopting flexible positions during the Cold War arose from its own basic decision to "moralize" its attitudes. The democracies portrayed the Cold War not as a possibly transient clash of competing interests but as a crisis of values based on immovable principles, like the war between the Sons of Light and the Sons of Darkness in the Dead Sea Scrolls. (Incidentally, the scrolls never divulged who came out as the winner in that epic confrontation.) When a rigorous ideological interpretation is given to a conflict of national interests, flexible responses become impossible. It is easier to compromise publicly between competing interests than between evil and virtue.

Successive governments in Israel had persuaded the public that the Palestinian nationalists led by the PLO were incurably devoted to the concept of Israel's "destruction." There came a period in which the PLO itself could not possibly have believed that Israel was destructible. Israel's military power had escalated to great power dimensions and its international relationships deprived the idea of Israel's destruction of any degree of credibility. On the other hand, the PLO had maneuvered itself by the early 1980s into military impotence. But the ridiculous legend of Israel's destructibility at the hands of the chronically weak Palestinians lived on in the Israeli public arena long after the Arab world regarded Israel as too powerful to be overcome. It took an Israeli election in 1992 with a sharp swing to the center to initiate a peace process, which brought Palestinians, Jordanians, and even Syrians to the negotiating table.

If the decision to engage the PLO in a peace negotiation had been made a few years earlier, many lives would have been saved and the complexities attending the negotiation would have been seriously diminished.

Israeli leaders eventually overcame their distrust of Yasir Arafat, the PLO leader, who had performed many murderous assaults on Israeli citizens over a long period. Prime Minister Yitzhak Rabin and Foreign Minister Shimon Peres showed commendable audacity in 1992 by deputing their juniors to negotiate an act of reconciliation with PLO leaders in Oslo. This led to a peace agreement which revolutionized the strategic balance in the Middle East.

When the negotiation began in, of all places, Oslo, it could not have proceeded very far without a veil of secrecy being drawn across it. If the Wilsonian dogma "no private diplomacy of any kind" had been obeyed, the peace agreements between Israel, Egypt, and Jordan and the strong Israeli links with Morocco, Tunisia, and some of the Gulf states would not have been concerted and the impulses in Israel and its Arab neighbors toward peaceful settlement would not have come to fulfillment. Here is clear evidence that secrecy is an essential element in progressing toward peaceful settlement of disputes.

Even when governments understand that they will have to modify their attitudes toward each other, it is important that they should have their own options about the timing of their concessions. In the Egyptian-Israeli negotiations, which have carried the Middle East toward a far lesser tension than ever before, both participants—Anwar Sadat of Egypt and Menachem Begin of Israel—offered far-reaching concessions which differed sharply from their previous positions. If they had merely reiterated their established attitudes, no agreements would ever have been possible. Begin had renounced all the Israeli-occupied territories, airfields, and oil resources in Sinai, and Sadat had virtually eliminated the traditional Egyptian hostility toward Israel. It was crucial that these reciprocal alleviations should be revealed as a package. If the concessions made by either of them had become known before publication of the advantages that each of them had gained, the peace treaty would never have been concluded. President Carter served an important international interest first by excluding the media from a detailed scrutiny of the developing accord, and then by insuring that the treaty could be presented as having positive effects for both of the contracting parties.

One way of securing acceptance for situations charged with great tension has been to delay public knowledge of crises until they have been surmounted. In the Cuban missile crisis it was helpful for the American people to know about President Kennedy's response at a time when he could announce that his formula had a good chance of acceptance. He declared that he would impose a blockade but would abstain from more drastic military initiatives. If the American public had been told of the immense risk its leader had taken at an earlier stage without also knowing the remedy for the crisis, it is possible that they would have been seized by the kind of panic that is not compatible with diplomatic solutions.

I do not wish to make a case for secrecy as a universal prescription. There have been occasions when courses were adopted which would never have been accepted in a context of public candor.

In February 1957 the *New York Times*'s Washington correspondent, James "Scotty" Reston, got wind of a proposal made to me as ambassador in Washington in an effort to secure the withdrawal of Israeli forces from Sinai after the Suez-Sinai war. If he had published his scoop immediately, my prime minister, David Ben-Gurion, would have heard it for the first time and might have rejected it publicly and irascibly. The result could have been the renewal of the Suez war.

Reston deferred publication at my request and never regretted his abstinence.

On the other hand, the intention of the United States under President Kennedy's leadership to invade Cuba in 1961 in an effort to subvert the Castro government became known to Reston. When the President approached Reston with a passionate request to avoid or, at least, to postpone publication, he spoke emotionally of the soldiers and sailors who might be put in risk. Reston patriotically acceded to Kennedy's request. The Bay of Pigs invasion was a debacle and the loss of prestige was totally disproportionate to the risks incurred. Reston subsequently regretted his failure to disclose the plan for the landing. If he had obeyed his journalistic interest, he might have saved his country from a humiliating failure. His published conclusion was that the news media ought to publish or broadcast any stories picked up about what governments were planning to do. Early publicity, he argued, might force them to proceed more thoughtfully.[5]

This case proved that the exercise of personal discretion by a journalist can sometimes be salutary, and sometimes not. Media pundits have to decide who they are; do they see themselves as mere commentators on events, come what may, or are they citizens like all others, with commitments to causes and partners in national destinies?

The utility of a secrecy option was made evident in a similar context when President Kennedy secretly sent former Secretary of State Dean Acheson to Paris to obtain President de Gaulle's support for the blockade of Cuba. It was believed that Western support of the United States would encourage Nikita Khrushchev to abandon his reckless incursion into the U.S. sphere of influence. If Acheson had been on a public mission and encountered a negative attitude in Paris, knowledge of a rift in allied unity would have demoralized the democratic world. On this occasion the French leader willingly sustained the U.S. policy and the result was a victory for Western power and prestige.

The debate on the role of publicity in international conflict ends with no generalized conclusion. Most historians and objective observers rejoice to know that American public opinion enabled U.S. extrication from the Vietnam War. The same observers regret that public opinion was prevented by secrecy from saving the Kennedy administration from its Bay of Pigs adventure in Cuba.

Most of us would applaud the fact that President Carter's insistence on secrecy in the Camp David Egyptian-Israeli talks made it possible for an agreement involving reciprocal compromises to be reached. Secrecy, together with a certain degree of procedural mendacity about Secretary of State Henry Kissinger's movements, helped the United States to heal its relations with China. Everybody would now agree that a Chinese-American understanding has contributed to international conciliation and stability. But those who applauded the results of secrecy in the American opening to China justifiably criticized the secrecy that led to the bombing of Cambodia during the Vietnam War.

It cannot be seriously doubted that the use of "back-channels" by Kissinger and the Soviet Union's ambassador in Washington, Alexei Dobrynin, contributed to the processes that led to the end of the Cold War. In his biography, Ambassador Dobrynin reveals that most of the important issues that he discussed with Kissinger were elaborated in a "back-channel" of which the official delegations of the United States were totally oblivious. Secret negotiation in remote and inaccessible places enables the parties to explore negotiating positions without becoming prematurely committed to "trial balloons."

There have been occasions when a totalitarian government was ready to do good by stealth. The Soviet government in the 1970s was under strong international pressure to facilitate the emigration of Soviet Jews who were held in virtual bondage in the USSR. It became ready, in its own interest, to allow more copious exit facilities than ever before. The Soviet advantage would consist of American readiness to reward Moscow with most favored nation status. The Soviets made secrecy a rigid condition without which the scheme would be aborted. It was one thing for the Soviet Union to appear in a positive light in the domain of human rights. It would be another matter for Moscow to appear as bargaining humiliatingly for a commercial concession.

When the benevolent compact was leaked to the media, Moscow closed the tap.

One reason for the success of the media lies in their capacity to fix the agenda of public preoccupation. In the early 1990s tragic starvation was rampant in many African countries. But harrowing portrayals of emaciated children happened to be most publicized in Somalia. The consequence was the arrival of a relatively massive U.S. military and humanitarian mission to Mogadishu, with an impressive panoply of renowned columnists and anchormen waiting on those bleak shores. It transpired that Somalia, with its ferocious warlords, was just about the least promising country for effective humanitarian action, and the anticlimax came with the ignominious flight of the humanitarians with nothing durable achieved.

International action in the Bosnian tragedy fluctuated depressingly in harmony with the media coverage and body count. While Sarajevo was afflicted by a horrifying slaughter of innocents, thousands of peacekeepers looked on for months with no capacity to intervene. When visual portrayal of terrorist bombardments with dozens of dead and maimed finally became unendurable at Western breakfast tables, NATO countries brought up aircraft carriers and bomber squadrons and went in with banners flying high.

It was when the outrage of "ethnic cleansing" became visual on television screens, with pitiful portrayals of masses moving away from their homes toward uncertain destinies, that negotiated settlements became possible. The pressure of visible anguish had more influence on the attainment of the historic Dayton accords than did the textual niceties of conferences.

The bottom line is that peace with secrecy may sometimes be preferable to secrecy without peace. There has never been a successful negotiation in which secrecy was not practiced at a crucial stage. We end with the frustrating truth that publicity has sometimes worked against useful international agreements, and on other occasions would have prevented costly international errors. There is nothing in the record to liberate statesmen from the necessity of choice.

My most emphatic conclusion about diplomacy is that there are no general solutions for particular cases.

It is unrealistic to expect political leaders to ignore public opinion. But a statesman who keeps his ear permanently glued to the ground will have neither elegance of posture nor flexibility of movement.

6 Where—If Not at the Summit?

The phrase "summit diplomacy," like much of our modern diplomatic vocabulary, goes back to Winston Churchill, not in his rhetorical glow during the Second World War, but in the greater lucidity and imaginativeness of his later career as prime minister in the 1950s.

Churchill had to overcome his lifelong anti-Communist passions and his own "iron curtain" speech in order to regard the death of Stalin as an opening to a dialogue with Stalin's successors. He thought that there was a prospect for what later became known as détente. "The idea appeals to me of a supreme effort to bridge the gulf between the two worlds, so that each can live their life, if not in friendship at least without the hatreds of the Cold War."[1]

Churchill went on to propose East-West negotiations at the highest level. Between 1955 and 1960, he proposed such negotiations on more than forty occasions. His persistence was resisted by many of his own colleagues and, especially, by leaders of the United States. There was even a churlish tendency to attribute his insistence to his advanced age and personal vanity. Nevertheless, he had coined a durable phrase in asking, "If there is not *at the summit* of the nations the wish to win the greatest prize of peace, where can men look for hope?"[2]

But while eloquence was Churchill's weapon, real power lay in Washington, where President Eisenhower was austerely reluctant to indulge in the dramatic temptations of summitry. In a recent book, Henry Kissinger suggests that Churchill was right and Eisenhower was wrong: the death of Stalin was followed by some Soviet gestures which might have given an opening for a tactical agreement. In Kissinger's appraisal: "During the war and for several years afterward, Churchill was far ahead of his time. Had he not lost the 1945 election, he might well have given the emerging Cold War a different direction."[3] Eisenhower believed that any accommodation with the Soviets should wait until the West was overpoweringly strong. Churchill thought that this point had been adequately achieved.

From Potsdam in 1945 to Geneva in 1955, no American President took part in a summit meeting. Moreover, the first summits in the 1950s were not very fertile. The major heads of state came together in Geneva in 1955, at Camp David in 1959, and in Paris in 1960. It would be hard to prove that they left the international scene in greater serenity than they found it. The reservations of professional and academic critics were consequently reinforced.

It seems, however, that skepticism about summitry is in direct proportion to the personal distance of the skeptic from the summit. Thus in 1957, when he was perched on the lower slopes, Kissinger could hold that many of the arguments advanced on behalf of summit meetings were "fatuous in the extreme." He argued that the proposition that only heads of state could settle intractable disputes was not borne out by experience. Problems of great complexity, which had divided the world for a decade and a half, were not likely to be resolved in a few days by harassed men meeting in the full light of publicity. He believed that summitry would give birth to a vogue of "intellectual frivolity, the evasion of concreteness, the reliance on personalities, the implication that all problems can be settled with one grand gesture."[4]

These arguments appear sound, but their fragility is illustrated by the speed with which they are relinquished whenever the theoretician becomes a practitioner. Kissinger's criticism of summitry vanished quickly when he himself qualified as the free world's most eminent and skillful negotiator. His virtuosity contributed to the opening to China as well as to the first disengagement stage of the Middle East peace process. He also orchestrated détente at a time when he was no less dominant than Presidents Ford and Nixon who confided in him. At that time I described Kissinger as "the only U.S. secretary of state under whom two presidents served."

During the first two hundred years of American history it was not always feasible for heads of state to oversee the transactions of their emissaries in any detail. The results of this gentle leash were seldom disastrous. Robert Livingston and James Monroe were empowered by President Thomas Jefferson to purchase New Orleans and West Florida from France for ten million dollars. They ended up buying half a continent for five million dollars, doubling the area of the United States by adding 820,000 square miles between the Mississippi and the Rocky Mountains. Most people today would judge this to be a successful real estate purchase. In the present age the two envoys might well have been rebuked in a telephone message from Washington, ordering them to stop fooling around with unauthorized expenditure, to stay within the limits of their instructions, and to avoid wasting money on extrabudgetary luxuries.

The most serious defect of summitry is its negative influence on the status and dignity of embassies. The plaintive protests of ambassadors against summiteering appear to be futile. As with the vogue of publicity, so with summitry: the best course is to abandon denunciation and bow to the inevitable. Negotiation at lower levels of authority was inevitable in the eras of limited communication simply because it was not feasible for sovereigns to meet each other frequently. In the early part of the eighteenth century, for example, a British prime minister, Sir Robert Peel, informed his colleagues in London that he had found a way of making the voyage from Rome to London in "a mere thirteen days." A journey from Boston to New York used to take four days. The highest rate of travel in those days was ten miles an hour. It is clear that in the era of six hundred miles an hour, it would be absurd for heads of government to behave as if the communications revolution had never occurred.

In my own research I have encountered a letter from President Jefferson to his secretary of state: "We have not heard from our ambassador in Spain for two years. If we do not hear from him this year—let us write him a letter." This splendid utterance reflects the pace of international business in a more tranquil epoch.

The first substantive change came with the invention of the telegraph, allowing home governments to give their ambassadors more precise instructions and to receive more exact information. Even then, however, monarchs, presidents, and foreign ministers could make their views and attitudes known by indirect influence rather than by personal contact. It was in World War II that summitry came into its own with the publicized and dramatic encounters of Roosevelt, Stalin, and Churchill. Yet even then, the hardships and hazards of prolonged travel were still so acute that each occasion gave hostages to fortune in the physical as well as in the diplomatic sense. Only the emergency of war could have impelled these elderly men and their leading associates to accept such frequent toil and risk. Today there is not very much risk and very little toil. There were times when ambassadors were really able to delude themselves with the conviction that they were "Envoys Extraordinary and Ministers Plenipotentiary," as their credentials claimed.

There is now a constant monarchization of government, under

which ambassadors, foreign ministers, and heads of governments carry the level of negotiation upward every year. The result is that policymakers are convinced that they no longer need so many intermediate levels of mediation. The heads of state do have a case. The wholesale deprecation of summitry is ill founded. The balance sheet of results is ambivalent. There have been occasions where summit meetings have left the international atmosphere even more disturbed than it was before. Such was the Khrushchev-Eisenhower-Macmillan-de Gaulle summit in Paris in 1960, which exploded on the U-2 issue. The Soviet leaders pretended to be surprised and disconcerted by evidence that the U.S. habitually inspected the air space of the Soviet Union. The real motive for Soviet indignation was the Kremlin's preference to await the election of a new U.S. President rather than negotiate deals with an incumbent on the verge of renouncing his office.

Yet it is difficult to believe that the errors ascribed to Yalta—delivering Eastern Europe into Stalin's hands—would have been avoided if the negotiators had not been heads of government. The American opening to China was only conceivable if it could be enacted conspiratorially at high levels of decision. The Camp David accords of 1979, with their sensational climax in an Egyptian-Israeli peace treaty, could never have been concluded without the intimacy of three leaders in secluded encounter, free from the pressures of domestic constituencies. Ostpolitik in 1976, culminating in the establishment of a security system in Europe, went forward at speed largely because it became the personal vocation of an authoritative head of government in the German Federal Republic. If Willy Brandt's efforts had been fragmented along routine lines, it is unlikely that they would have reached success.

Summit meetings have now lost their emergency character. They are not confined to functional necessities: they have also taken over the symbolic and ceremonial domain of diplomacy.

Up to the end of the 1930s it was possible for a statesman to be a prime minister even of Britain or France without ever having met a President of the United States. This was actually the case with Neville Chamberlain, who never met Franklin D. Roosevelt. Today, a pilgrimage to major countries—especially Washington—is the first care of an elected, appointed, or self-appointed leader. The heads of state and government in other major capitals such as Moscow, London, Paris, Bonn, and Rome can all expect to receive from a dozen to a score of their opposite numbers every year. There is a personal acquaintanceship among them, similar to that which used to prevail among "the royal cousins" in European courts. Some writers have feared that this climate of affability works against objective analysis. Harold Nicolson has written: "Diplomacy is the art of negotiating *documents* in a ratifiable and therefore dependable form. It is by no means the art of conversation. . . . Diplomacy, if it is ever to be effective, should be a disagreeable business. And one recorded in hard print."[5]

The best argument for summitry, apart from its inevitability, is the integral character of modern diplomacy. When negotiations are held at a departmental level, representatives are limited by their departmental status. They are each in charge of a particular sector of the national responsibility, and cannot offer package deals. On the other hand, heads of government can trade an economic concession for a military advantage or a diplomatic gain.

Paradoxically, if summitry has its dangers, these are reduced by multiplication. When a summit meeting was rare, conspicuous, and dramatic, there was a chance that its failure would generate deadlock or despair. A device that was designed to alleviate world tensions would end up by aggravating them. Now that summit meetings have become prosaic and even routinized,[6] their failures, if not too frequent or drastic, can be absorbed without shock.

In any case, decisions about the frequency of summit meetings depend on the personal inclinations of the world leaders. The

lack of superpower summitry between 1945 and 1955 was because Truman and Eisenhower tended to rely on strong secre-
taries of state, Dean Acheson and Foster Dulles. When I was
Israel's ambassador in Washington for nine years, I received only
one visit from my prime minister, David Ben-Gurion, although
important negotiations were carried on in both my embassies—
in Washington and the United Nations. Ben-Gurion was totally
unimpressed by the ceremonial fuss of summit meetings, and was
an artist in the delegation of authority.

Most of the adverse criticism of summitry comes from professional diplomats in the press and the professional literature. The
principal accusation is of superficiality arising out of haste. There
is no time for the careful, meticulous study of problems.

But the denunciation of summit meetings would be more
convincing if it were confirmed by case histories. One of the
difficulties in the controversy about summit meetings arises from
the ambiguity surrounding the ideas of success and failure. What
do these words mean?

The critics of summit meetings appear to believe that success
has something to do with amiability. Thus, if the encounter of
powerful leaders ends up on a contentious note, it is assumed that
injury has been done to the international cause. This may not
necessarily be the case. A frank knowledge of difficulties arising
from the conflicting temperaments and personal traits of leaders
might be a useful result, even if it creates a somber atmosphere. It
did no great harm for President Kennedy in Vienna in 1961 to
become aware of the dark and threatening side of Khrushchev's
character, or for the Soviet leader to discern that behind the
young President's layer of inexperience was a hard sense of power
and resolve. The idea that a summit meeting is successful only if it
ends in fatuous declarations of harmony ought surely to have died
a permanent death after the Munich conference in 1938.

Some serious scholars believe that the coldly grim and formidable impression left by de Gaulle on Khrushchev before the

aborted Paris summit meeting in 1960 may have tipped the balance against a Soviet move on Berlin.

Israeli leaders who have met Yasir Arafat have usually found him to be a serious interlocutor with attributes common to many of those who have passed from revolutionary violence to an understanding of the compulsions that drive former foes to a searching exploration of a peaceful future. This happened to Arafat's relations even with Israeli Prime Minister Yitzhak Rabin, who was more frugal in the distribution of praise than anyone I have ever met. Rabin ended his life believing that Arafat was a viable partner for implementing the Oslo accords.

An important attribute for any emissary of peace, official or personal, is to know in any country where real power lies. When President Carter visited me in Israel a few years ago, he was pursued by adverse publicity in Damascus, where it was noted that he would spend three days in Israel and had spent only a few hours in the Syrian capital. The answer that he gave to me was convincing: "In order to get a feeling about Israeli decisionmaking, you have to speak to fifteen people there. In Damascus it is necessary to speak to one person alone."

One of the consequences of summitry is, of course, the decline of the ambassadorial function. By the time that Roosevelt and Churchill established their summitry practice in World War II, the efficacy of foreign offices had already been eroded through constant interference by political leaders. The French and British governments ignored accurate and ominous reports reaching them through normal diplomatic channels. Heads of government felt, then as now, that they were born with a special genius for diplomacy and had no need for the tedious, pedantic warnings of experts.

Across the Channel, in the autumn of 1935, French diplomats were sending predictions to Paris about an imminent German reoccupation of the Rhineland. And three years later—in October 1938, after the Munich agreement—the French ambassador in Moscow, Robert Coulondre, was reporting that a Russian rapprochement with Germany could be expected. Gordon Craig admits that it is not clear whether these reports ever reached the decisionmakers. What does seem clear is that statesmen often give their confidence only to reports which match their preconceived notions and their wishful thinking.[7]

The possibility of a German-Russian rapprochement across the ideological divide was such an improbable idea in 1938–1939 that it would have been normal to dismiss it as a nightmare fantasy. But political leaders could have been expected to give it a few days of examination.

There is a functional relationship between the complacency of political leaders and the more skeptical rigor of foreign offices. Bad news is generally not something that politicians want to hear. Their natural reaction is to resent the bearer of evil tidings, and to punish him for disturbing their serenity. A more sophisticated device is to dismiss the diplomat's nervousness as a sign of weak character or inadequate national feeling.

Some diplomats have cooperated in the decline of their profession by obsequiously sacrificing truth on the altar of popularity. When they do this they become a danger to their own peoples. Thus, in the late 1930s, the British ambassador in Berlin, Neville Henderson, strove mightily to console his masters in London with the idea that Hitler's appetite would really stop short at Czechoslovakia and that he would not go on to attack Poland as well. That is what Chamberlain at first wanted to hear. When Hitler actually marched into Prague, even Chamberlain believed that war was inevitable, but then the interval for preparation was desperately short.

Fortunately, totalitarian diplomacy is even more prone to these illusions. In the early part of World War II, the Nazi German ambassador in Dublin was comforting Hitler with reports that Churchill was unpopular in England and would soon be succeeded by a leader willing to compromise with nazism. This fantasy seems to have played a part in causing Hitler to delay the launching of what might well have been a successful invasion of the British Isles. What was the point of accepting all that risk if British resolve was going to collapse on its own accord?

The American ambassador in London in the early part of World War II, Joseph P. Kennedy, described Britain with such hostile contempt that his dispatches must have strengthened all those in the United States who believed that it would be worthless for America to invest its strength and fidelity in what Kennedy was describing as a lost cause. Fortunately, Roosevelt ignored that advice and received more favorably the reports of his special assistant, Harry Hopkins.

But while governments may sometimes have suffered through taking too much notice of ambassadors, a greater affliction has arisen from taking too little notice of them. A prominent example is the refusal of Western governments to believe their ambassadors in Teheran, who were convinced in the late 1970s that the shah's regime was more insecure than the legend of "Iranian stability" would allow them to believe. Former Under Secretary of State George Ball has written, "Not only was the State Department being excluded from the management of our policies toward Iran, [in 1978] I soon found out that our ambassador in Teheran, a seasoned career officer, William H. Sullivan, was being similarly bypassed."[8]

One of the handicaps of diplomacy is that while it is admired as a profession, it is not yet plugged into any recognized science. It cannot intimidate the amateurs by requiring them to prove their credentials after a specific training process. Ernest Bevin is said to have remarked that the only job he could ever have obtained in the British Foreign Office was that of foreign secretary; he could never have become a junior officer or a fourth secretary, since these posts were subject to examinations in history and French.

The shaping of high policy is now moving away from the embassies. Few ambassadors claim to be filling as formidable a role as in the past. There has been an enormous growth in the world's diplomatic community as a result of the proliferation of states and the functional expansion of themes that fall under the headings of international relations. Up to World War II, the number of people bearing full ambassadorial titles could be counted in the hundreds. Today, by a rough estimate, there are sixty thousand officials in the world exercising diplomatic functions in foreign offices, embassies, and international organizations. Yet an increase in numbers has been accompanied by a sharp decline in influence and prestige.

A great deal of truth is contained in the verdict of Hedley Bull: "The decline of professional diplomacy may prove to be both a cause and a result of a wider decline in the conditions of international order in this century."[9]

Whatever changes take place in diplomacy, the professional ambassador is the loser on all fronts. His political masters do much of the negotiation and usurp some of his symbolic function in celebrating and dramatizing international friendships. Miniature foreign ministries spring up in prime ministers' offices, and in the United States a new layer of intervention interposes itself between policymakers and embassies through national security advisors and personal representatives of Presidents.

The diplomacy of the United States was enriched in the 1960s by scholars and writers such as the liberal economist John Kenneth Galbraith. One of the benefits of allowing outsiders to penetrate a professional domain is that it allows the transient members to reveal some of the secrets of the guild. Galbraith must have discomfited many career diplomats by exposing the inequalities of their burdens. Not all of them are equally hard-working. Galbraith writes, "In India during my time there were some fifty ambassadors. . . . They were a spectacular example of what economists . . . call disguised unemployment. The ambassadors from

Argentina or Brazil could not have had more than a day's serious work a month. The more deeply engaged diplomats from Scandinavia, Holland, Belgium or Spain could discharge their essential duties in one day a week."[10]

The myth of the valuable cocktail party also crumbles before the corrosive pen. "I never learned anything at a cocktail party or dinner that I didn't already know, needed to know or wouldn't soon have learned in the normal course of business. The emphasis that diplomats of all countries in all capitals accord to entertaining is the result of a conspiracy by which function is found in pleasant social intercourse and controlled inebriation."[11]

It would be much fairer on this point to draw attention to the fire-brigade role of embassies. After months of routine and lethargy, a crisis can erupt which places an ambassador in the center of a sudden turmoil. It is also distressingly true that in the course of their service, ambassadors and their colleagues have often been afflicted by tragic personal sacrifice in their countries' cause.

In the present populist mood of public opinion, professional diplomats are not going to find much help outside their embattled embassies. They can only look back with nostalgic wonder to the time when the mission headed by Benjamin Franklin, from his legation in a Paris suburb, negotiated the adherence of France to the fight of the American colonies against George III. And when a British ambassador of dominating temperament in Constantinople, Stratford Canning, made a personal decision to warn all concerned that Britain would fight against Russia or Austria if either of them attacked Turkey. He gave this guarantee because it would have taken him at least two months to explain the whole issue by courier to and from London. Since no war did break out between Turkey, Russia, and Austria, nobody can prove that the daring ambassador did not pull off a successful operation of deterrence.

No ambassador is likely to have such a sense of power again. Modern international relations are a pragmatic business, closely anchored to the needs and hopes of contemporary society. It is therefore gratifying to note that the stilted forms of credential ceremonies, the residual use of glitter in the diplomatic uniforms, as well as the obsession with precedents and titles are becoming obsolete. Simplification is already at work among the political and diplomatic representatives of the fifteen countries which are members of the European Union. The very frequency of their meetings would make it impossible or at least tedious and absurd for them to go through all the formalities that were traditionally associated with international exchanges. The sacrifice of mystique is rewarded by a deeper public understanding of the real, concrete interests which diplomacy seeks to serve.

Diplomatic relations are not a grace to be conferred but a convenience to be used. Nothing is more absurd than the "breaking off" of diplomatic relations in moments of crisis. It is precisely when there is conflict that there is most need of such relations, and yet it is in such conditions that they are often sundered.

Between 1917 and 1934 the United States denied itself relations of any kind with the Soviet Union. The question whether the Soviets would have been influenced by American political culture cannot be answered. The United States, interpreting diplomatic ties as a reward for good conduct or a penalty for misdemeanor, was excluding any prospect of balancing the policies of two vast nations one against the other. Then, for many years the United States denied itself the opportunity of conducting its dialogue with China through the diplomatic channel. This behavior reflected the erroneous belief that diplomatic relations have a moral rather than a utilitarian significance. How the United States and the Soviet Union might have interacted with each other immediately after World War I belongs to a world of hypothetical speculation.

During the 1967 Arab-Israeli war, the Soviet Union decided to break its relations with Israel. When its ambassador came to see me, then a very recently appointed foreign minister, he delivered a hostile tirade, ending with the phrase that "since there is a conflict of policy between the Soviet Union and Israel, my government has decided to break relations." Never having experienced such a hostile assault by a major nuclear power, I took refuge in rationality. I said, "If our policies are as divergent as you say, surely we should *increase* our diplomatic relations, *deepen* them, put more people to work, write *more* memoranda to each other."

His reply was unforgettable: "What Your Excellency is saying is logical, but I have not come here to be logical, I have come here to break relations with Israel."

The consequence of the Soviet rupture of relations with Israel was that the Soviet Union, having no discourse with one of the parties in the Middle East, lost all possibilities of influence. It had awarded the monopoly of influence to the United States. Soviet emotion and Soviet interest had collided with each other, and emotion had won.

When all is said and done, diplomacy is a profession like other professions. It becomes less awe-inspiring the more that is known about it. It has to be empirical, pragmatic, and intuitive, since it cannot rest its assumptions on any rigorous mathematics. It depends in the last resort on the way in which its practitioners react to opportunities and dangers as they arise.

There is no effective substitute for the exercise of trained professional minds by those who understand the attitudes of other nations in their full complexity. These qualities require constant immersion in the daily life of a foreign society, which cannot be acquired in a brief descent of statesmen from aircraft for a few hectic days. The kind of subterranean rumblings which often precede changes of power can only be discerned by those who have had prolonged contact with the countries of their accreditation. Sometimes an official at a lower hierarchical level can, by sheer assiduity, achieve results that a rushed visit by a head of state would be unable to emulate. Richard Holbrooke proved this in negotiating the Serb-Croatian-Bosnian accord concluded at Dayton, Ohio, and if there is a breakthrough in the Middle East peace process, it will owe much to the patience and assiduity of the American envoy Dennis Ross.

Nothing should prevent statesmen from using their authority at the summit, but it would be internationally harmful if professional diplomats were to lose their sense of vocation through being constantly outflanked by their political masters.

7 Still Too Many Wars

Nothing is more fallacious than to deduce nuclear conclusions from nonnuclear precedents. It is true that nations have always regarded certain interests and causes as superior to peace, but when a particular form of war becomes not only murderous but suicidal, a list of objectives that can rationally be regarded as worth the risk of nuclear attack becomes so drastically reduced that reference to the past is inoperative. Nuclear weaponry is a break in the continuity of history. It threatens a result in which victory and defeat have been drained of their meaning.

The fact that the United States and the Soviet Union avoided using any of their thousands of nuclear warheads after 1945 sounds like a victory for moral impulses and ethical insight. It would be more convincing to regard it as a recognition of reciprocal self-interest. The danger of nuclear confrontation undoubtedly moderated the behavior of the two superpowers. Each nation drew the same conclusions from the specter of nuclear warfare: neither would be spared in the ensuing holocaust. The dilemma of the nuclear era had been described by J. Robert

Oppenheimer, one of the pioneers of the atomic era, who called the superpowers "two scorpions in a bottle."

The fact that bombs with nuclear warheads were actually used at Hiroshima and Nagasaki seemed to confirm the deterministic view that all weapons invented are destined to be used. This idea, however, was discredited by the circumstance that one country, the United States, had an atomic monopoly. In 1945, the option of demonstrating an atomic bomb without its actual use was not taken as seriously as it would have to be in the 1950s and thereafter.[1] In 1945, there was also no restraining fear of retaliation. Therefore, President Truman's decisionmaking process in 1945 is not a viable point of departure for estimating the likelihood of a similar decision later.

It is hard to believe that Truman's decision would have been taken so firmly if Japan had been capable of withstanding a first strike and returning nuclear fire. It can be argued that what made Hiroshima possible was not the existence of nuclear weapons but the lack of any retaliatory capacity at the disposal of Japan.

Once the two nuclear giants had an equal capacity to destroy the planet, the survival of mankind became dependent not on a realistic prospect of nuclear war but on the effectiveness of deterrence and the avoidance of miscalculation or surprise attack. Deterrence means that you have to threaten the use of weapons that you don't want to use in order to avoid using them. For deterrence to succeed, there must be three conditions: the existence of power, the readiness to use it, and the reflection of these two facts in the consciousness of the potential adversary. If the power exists and there is no belief in its usability, the deterrent effect is in abeyance.

Yet the countries that possess nuclear weapons have felt safer than those who do not. The porcupine is not a cuddlesome bed partner, but it has a good prospect of not being easily devoured.

The pessimists might declare that, even in the era of balance, a nuclear war was an evident possibility during the Cuban missile crisis of 1962, so that something that nearly happened should not be dismissed as impossible even now. The answer is that the exemplary effects of the Cuban missile crisis were more likely to serve both parties as warnings than as models for emulation. There is also reason to doubt whether the nuclear factor was really decisive in determining that crisis. An American authority has convincingly concluded: "Our supremacy in conventional and naval forces . . . had more to do with the successful outcome of the crisis than our overwhelming superiority in strategic nuclear weaponry."[2]

More serious was the danger that a power facing defeat in conventional war would, in desperation, make use of its nuclear superiority in order to recapture the military initiative. The candidate for this unenviable role was the United States. On at least three occasions, American commanders sent memoranda to President Johnson and Secretary of Defense McNamara urging them to consider options of a nuclear attack on North Vietnam. On March 2, 1964, the U.S. military chiefs suggested that the nuclear option be used in the event that China came to the aid of Hanoi.[3] McNamara has written: "The president and I were shocked by the almost cavalier way in which the chiefs and their associates on this and other occasions referred to, and accepted the risk of, the possible use of nuclear weapons. Apart from the moral issues raised by nuclear strikes, initiating such action against a nuclear equipped opponent is almost surely an act of suicide. I do not want to exaggerate the risks associated with the chiefs' views, but I believe that even a low risk of a catastrophic event must be avoided. That lesson had not been learned in 1964. I fear neither our nation nor the world has fully learned it to this day."[4]

McNamara writes that three years later, on May 20, 1967, the chiefs "sent me another memo repeating their view that invasions of North Vietnam, Laos and Cambodia might become necessary involving . . . quite possibly the use of nuclear weapons in southern China."[5]

These memos by the military leaders in the United States are an antidote to the facile assurance that there was never any danger of nuclear explosions during the Cold War. The unexpected truth is that the power which came nearest to initiating a nuclear exchange in the Vietnam crises was none other than the United States.

The balance of terror, or the "balance of prudence," as the French scholar Raymond Aron preferred to call it, had the advantage of being self-implementing. It did not depend on written agreements or institutions. It operated through the intrinsic self-interest of the parties. It presupposed enough rationality to preclude suicidal adventure. But even if there was an unwritten agreement to maintain the nuclear balance without war, there was still great need for preventive measures to avoid miscalculations and surprise.

A complex system of measures for avoiding war by misunderstanding was concerted by the nuclear powers. They included direct communication between the leaders of the superpowers, reciprocal advance notice of maneuvers and troop movements, military missions in each superpower capital, and abstention from bomber flights in areas or periods of tension. This system seemed able to absorb and neutralize areas of miscalculation. The melancholy view that a single nuclear weapon would inevitably start the entire chain of universal destruction underestimated the will and capacity of the nuclear powers to halt a process before it passed beyond control.

There has always been an intellectual gap between the accumulation of nuclear weapons and the growth of understanding about their significance. There were some years during which the United States had a monopoly of nuclear power, but there is

no evidence that this caused Washington to follow policies different from those that it would otherwise have espoused. The democratic value system seemed to forbid any policy of vulgar threat
and intimidation by the United States toward its adversaries.

But the fact that nuclear bombs were not used does not mean
that the nuclear arms had no influence. There has been no dimi-
nution of the political or psychological deployment of nuclear
arms. The United States and the Soviet Union—and, to a lesser
extent, Britain, France, and China—sometimes brandished their
nuclear arsenals openly in order to assert their status and to
downplay other elements of their vulnerability.

Far from regarding the nuclear fear as an incentive to abolition
or even reduction, the powers have made a virtue of necessity by
emphasizing the positive stabilizing and deterrent role of nuclear
arsenals. Churchill was able to declare, as early as March 1949: "It
is certain . . . that Europe would have been communized [like
Czechoslovakia] and London would have been under bombardment some time ago, but for the deterrent of the atomic bomb in
the hands of the United States."[6] He also coined the memorable
phrase that "safety would prove to be the sturdy child of terror."
Churchill never faltered in his conviction that the nuclear balance
was a source of universal comfort and that the anguish that it
provoked was irrational.

Without a single bomb having been dropped since Nagasaki,
the very existence of the weapon has revolutionized the way in
which governments have thought about war and international
relations. The paradox which tells us that military force has become both more dangerous and less usable than ever before has
brooded over contemporary diplomacy and defined its tone and
mood. A new academic discipline with its own vocabulary and
logistic routines has replaced the previous strategic jargon.

While the nuclear powers never lacked arguments for maintaining their nuclear arsenals, there is some mystery about the
importance they attached to numerical proliferation. The notion

that the two major superpowers could maintain a nuclear balance at an immensely lower quantitative level is the kind of simple truth that becomes self-evident as soon as it is enunciated. The objective is balance, not any particular quantity beyond the capacity to inflict vast destruction. Yet this simple veracity has been lost from view in the absurd talk about "parity," "superiority," and "who is ahead of whom."

It is certifiably true that a country that has five thousand tanks is objectively "stronger" than a country which has only two thousand. But this arithmetical logic has no place whatever in the nuclear context. It is simply untrue that a power which has the capacity to destroy the planet a million times over is "stronger" than a power that could destroy the planet only half a million times.

On one occasion, Secretary of State Kissinger raised the despairing cry: "What is meant by superiority? What is the use of it? What can one do with it?" But this rationality seemed to have no visible effect on the resolution of the United States to prevent what President Kennedy called "a missile gap" which never really existed. Thus, the proliferation of nuclear weapons became tools in a game of prestige in which the stakes were almost totally fictitious.

Diplomacy here faces another paradox: it used to be thought that there was a direct relationship between the avoidance of war and the solution of problems that provoked tensions. This is no longer self-evident. The nuclear age has not offered strong incentives for radical conflict resolution, and neither does the present post–Cold War situation. Governments do not now seem inclined to adopt the painful compromises required to solve conflicts. They take refuge in the thought that the balance of prudence will prevent major conflagration, even if they leave basic problems unresolved. It seems to have been proved, since the end of the Cold War, that the nuclear age is more congenial to partial or interim settlements than to radical solutions.

By strange anomaly, the unfeasibility of using nuclear weapons ultimately became a primary motive for ending the Cold War. Since the two major nuclear powers were compelled to cooperate for the avoidance of nuclear war, it seemed logical for them to cooperate for the avoidance of war altogether. To this we must add the undoubted reality that the task of maintaining an escalating nuclear balance reduced one of the partners—the Soviet Union—to exhaustion verging on impotence.

A complicating factor in the nuclear debate has been the claim of one of the parties to moral superiority. Movements for the renunciation of nuclear arsenals sent hundreds of thousands marching in demonstrations, mostly in Europe. The defect of this agitation lies in the fact that its sponsors could only promote the abandonment of nuclear arms by the democracies. The Soviet nuclear weaponry was impervious to antinuclear demonstrations in London, Paris, and Stockholm. I find it hard to understand why the prevention of war by effective deterrence was more moral than the invitation of war by avoidable imbalance. After all, the Second World War was the result not of armaments but of disarmament. Those who were prepared to accept existing stabilities or to negotiate changes in them allowed their own strength to erode, leaving the aggressors in possession of the field.[7]

Yet the climax in the nuclear story is sardonically optimistic: it finds the nuclear powers beginning to dismantle their systems, leaving a few dissident but not very powerful states to face their suicidal choices in solitude.

With the end of the Cold War, the impossibility of a nuclear exchange between superpowers has been taken for granted, and attention has shifted sharply to "rogue states." These, by common definition, are states that combine nuclear capacity with hegemonic aspirations. They are set on regional domination while pursuing nuclear, biological, and chemical weapons capacity.

According to a Pentagon definition, fifteen developing states will eventually have a capacity to produce ballistic missiles, and eight of these are probably close to nuclear weapon capacity.

The United States, which is the central power among the states opposing nuclear weapons proliferation, does not accord the unenviable "rogue" title to all the states deemed to possess nuclear capacity or to be close to it. Israel's reputation for nuclearity has won the indulgence of the United States, which has rejected an Egyptian demand for the nuclear disarmament of Israel. The United States, whose relations with Israel under the Clinton regime have become closer than those with any other country, believes that a comprehensive peace with the Arab states is a justifiable Israeli condition for such a measure on Israel's part. In this respect, the United States is applying in practice the very balance of power doctrine which it disavows in theory.

An authoritative work published in the United States enumerates five rogue states (Iraq, Iran, Libya, North Korea, and Syria) and seven prospective rogues (China, India, Pakistan, Egypt, South Korea, Taiwan, and Turkey).[8]

This net appears to me to be spread too wide. Turkey is not recognized as a country aiming at nuclear capacity. Syria is generally regarded as incapable technologically of such a status. There are countries of undoubted capacity in this field, such as Canada, Switzerland, and Sweden, whose policies do not evoke anxiety in Washington or anywhere else. There has been good progress in the denuclearization of Ukraine; this seems to indicate a Russian decision to abandon nuclear pretensions.

The scenarios in which a nuclear exchange could probably erupt are thus relatively limited: they would include such contingencies as a North Korean attempt to intimidate or attack South Korea; Iranian attempts to threaten Israel from its stockpile of chemical weapons; a renewed Iraqi effort to annex or threaten Kuwait or Israel; the intimidation of Egypt or Israel by Libya; and the possibility of an outbreak of violence between India and Pakistan.[9]

The action of the French government in forcing nuclear tests on a peaceful South Pacific coast illustrates the power of inertia and momentum. Nuclear activity is too closely linked with other techniques for us to believe that it will come to an abrupt end. As years went by after Hiroshima and Nagasaki, the manufacture and deployment of nuclear materials became a matter of lineage, prestige and, in a few cases, security.

The United States, the champion of nonproliferation, is unlikely to press Israel to sign the Nuclear Nonproliferation Treaty (NPT) so long as Iran, Iraq, and Libya present credible threats to Israel's security. It is doubtful if India or Pakistan will change its present attitude in the absence of some spectacular act of reconciliation between them. The United States has shown no signs of believing that North Korea has already suspended its nuclear development.

There is still no unanimity in the West about the prospect of the nonproliferation campaign waged by the United States. A recently published book presents a debate between two authorities on strategic problems. Kenneth N. Waltz, professor of political science at the University of California, Berkeley, says: "The more nuclear weapons, the better." Scott O. Sagan, assistant professor at Stanford, replies: "More would be worse." Intermediate between the two are those who believe that American efforts to stem the tide of nuclear advance are unlikely to succeed, so that the necessity to choose between the two appraisals would be a waste of time and effort.

Waltz's case is inspired by precedents. He points out that the two superpowers maintained a long peace throughout the Cold War, despite deep political hostilities, numerous crises, and a prolonged arms race. Sagan replies that this complacency takes inadequate note of the possibility that governments do not always behave rationally.

Although nuclear weapons are less likely to be used now than they ever were, there is no possibility that they will disappear from history, like cavalry horses or pruning hooks and spears. The idea of nonproliferation will compete with a fatalistic understanding that our world will have to go on living with most of the nonconventional weaponry that now exists.

It is the unenviable vocation of the Middle East to be the main or sole area in which the possibility of a nuclear strike cannot be excluded. The danger arises not from the existence of Iran, Iraq, and Libya but from their attitudes and policies. Libya has taken its anti-Israeli posture to extreme lengths. It has even provoked an American threat to attack a center where the United States suspects activity supporting the manufacture of chemical weapons. Iran is consumed by a fundamentalist Islamic ideology and is regarded by Israel, and even by the United States, as a major source of the terrorist activities which have tormented the Middle East since Ayatollah Khomeini triumphed in the power struggle in Teheran.

Iraq irresponsibly sent Scud missiles against Israeli and Saudi Arabian targets during the Gulf War. A bombardment by Israeli air forces of the Osiris reactor near Baghdad may no longer be repeatable, given the habit of nuclear powers to disperse the various elements of their nuclearity. Former Prime Minister Shimon Peres, who introduced Israel into the world of high technology and nuclear deterrence, never supported the Osiris operation, presumably because he did not wish to approve a precedent for an exchange of nuclear fire in the Middle East. He relied on the assumption that the French government, headed by François Mitterand, which had constructed the reactor would deny Iraq the capacity to make it active.

Whether or not it is palatable to the rest of the world, Israel's perceived nuclear capacity has undoubtedly had a deterrent and therefore a stabilizing effect on the international balance. The only viable substitutes would be a revolutionary change in the attitudes of Iran and Iraq toward Israel, such as Egypt and a number of other Arab states have undergone. Or, alternatively, a successful U.S. attempt to induce all the Middle Eastern states to embark on a nonproliferation policy, which would require meticulous supervision and safeguards.

Until either one of these options is accepted, it will be unrealistic to believe that the threat of the nuclear mushroom cloud has already been blown away from the Middle East.

It used to be thought that the end of the nuclear era would automatically be accompanied by a general reduction in the use of military force. This was never a rational assumption and has now been disproved by events. The relationship between nuclear and conventional force is marked by inverse proportion. The certainty that nuclear weaponry is virtually neutralized creates a sense of impunity for the increased use of conventional power. One of the inhibiting factors in the use of conventional weapons was the fear that a "normal" conflict might spontaneously develop into a nuclear exchange. During the Cold War any power which felt that its interests would be advanced by military action did not hesitate to use it. There is no universally accepted restraint against military intervention.

In a brilliantly documented and admirably concise book on this problem, Richard Haass lists the military interventions of the recent decades: "A quick sample would include Turkey in Cyprus; Cuba in Angola; the Soviet Union in Hungary, Czechoslovakia, and Afghanistan; China in Vietnam; Vietnam in Cambodia; both Israel and Syria in Lebanon; India in Pakistan (giving rise to Bangladesh) and then again in the Maldives and Sri Lanka; and Great Britain against Argentina in the Falklands/Malvinas conflict."[10]

These outbreaks are listed by Haass in addition to the military initiatives of the United States. American forces operated against

Iran in 1979 to liberate hostages; in Lebanon in 1982, where eighteen hundred marines plus four thousand French, Italian, and British troops were invited after a horrifying massacre of Palestinian refugees by Christian Phalangists, with indirect Israeli presence in the area; in Grenada to protect American lives; against Libya to punish that country for involvement in terrorism; in Saudi Arabia and Kuwait to expel Iraqi forces that had invaded Kuwait; in the Philippines to defend the Corazon Aquino regime against an attempted rebel putsch; in former Yugoslavia to protect the Muslims in Bosnia and later to participate in a peacekeeping force charged with implementing a Serb-Croatian-Bosnian settlement concluded at Dayton, Ohio; in Somalia to combat famine; in Haiti to uphold the elected Aristides administration and to promote democracy.

If we go back to the 1970s, which Haass's study does not do, the assault on Israel by Egypt and Syria in 1973 was remarkable for the immense dimensions and destructive power of the weaponry that was used. It was rumored that more tanks were engaged in Golan and Sinai than had fought at Stalingrad. This reminds us that there are now small and medium-sized countries which have military forces of the kind that used to belong only to the great imperial and continental powers.

None of the wars in Haass's list, except that in former Yugoslavia, was pursued uninterruptedly for long periods. In none of them did a victorious party aspire to the unconditional surrender of its adversary. The Gulf War in 1990 surpassed all the other outbreaks of military action since the Yom Kippur war of 1973. Despite the depressingly large number of occasions when nations decided for war, it is possible to discern a certain hesitancy that inhibited or curtailed the exercise of such options. The general rule has been that expressed by the notion of limited war. By this I mean wars in which both parties use less than their total forces to achieve less than the total destruction of their adversaries. If war has any logic at this turn of the millennium it lies in its tendency to create conditions for diplomatic settlements, not in its potential for unlimited slaughter.

The countries that went to war in the past few decades showed great versatility in the justifications that they invoked. The classic definition of just war, formulated by Walzer, is that "states may use military force in the face of threats of war, whenever the failure to do so would seriously risk their territorial integrity or political independence. Under such circumstances it can fairly be said that they have been forced to fight and that they are the victims of aggression."[11]

Very few of the wars listed above met this austere criterion. The territorial integrity or political independence of the Soviet Union was not "at risk" in the Soviet invasions of Hungary or Czechoslovakia, nor was that of the United States during the entry of American troops into the Dominican Republic and former Yugoslavia. It was said of the Prussian leader Frederick the Great that when he planned a war he would convene his generals first and his legal adviser afterward. Even democratic governments contemplating war rarely considered questions of legality before they plunged into military action.

It is true that article 51 of the UN Charter speaks of the "inherent right of individual or collective self-defense if an armed attack occurs against a Member of the United Nations." But governments stretch the idea of self-defense so broadly as to cover almost any plea of a security threat. The British and French forces invading Egypt in temporary alliance with Israel in 1956 stated that their action was legitimized by the decision of President Nasser to close the Suez Canal. Keeping a canal under international governance must be reckoned as the least convincing defense ever given to a warlike initiative. It would have served their cause better to describe the British and French action truthfully as a typical "balance of power" war in preparation for a probable denial of vital European interests. Israel alone was entitled to invoke the security argument, since Egypt and other Arab states did assert a right of belligerency against Israel.

The fact that the wars discussed in this chapter were rarely prolonged and were severely localized does not dispose of the truth that they were very numerous and that the sum total of their victims was poignantly high. Manfred Halpern correctly explains: "One major reason why there is not yet a controlling international sense of morality is that the world does not yet share a single structure of knowledge, values and sanctions."[12]

This cheerless truth, together with the record of many superfluous wars, indicates that there is little hope that our generation will ever see an internationally accepted definition of legitimate and illegitimate interventions.

8 The United Nations: No "New Order"—Yet

The most sensational military action in the 1990s was the Gulf War. The United States dispatched a vast expeditionary force to Saudi Arabia, headed by 540,000 Americans, in a successful attempt to liberate Kuwait from the invading Iraqi occupiers.

The legal and ethical background for this action was exceptionally congenial to the United States and its allies. Kuwait was a sovereign state and a member of the United Nations. The attempt to destroy its independence was a classic instance of aggression, similar to Hitler's conquest of Poland and all the major capitals of Europe in World War II. There was none of the ambivalence that had attended the American military actions in Vietnam. No one could portray the United States as intruding into a "civil war." The success of President George Bush and Secretary of State James Baker in obtaining the endorsement of the UN Security Council allayed the apprehensions of Americans and Europeans about the legitimacy of their action. The United States deployed its forces under Generals Colin Powell and Norman Schwarzkopf with dazzling efficiency. It mobilized the full resources of its technology on land, on sea, and especially in the air. The casualties of the UN forces were minimal—no more than three hundred. Iraq suffered great civilian loss as a result of aerial bombardments, but its armies avoided annihilation by the speed of their surrender.

An unusual factor in this action was its endorsement by the Soviet Union under Mikhail Gorbachev's leadership. This would have been entirely inconceivable at any time during the Cold War. The abstention of China in the Security Council vote was another windfall for the United States.

The American cause was favored by the unpopularity of the Iraqi leader, Sadam Hussein. He is well described in a phrase used by a British historian about Philip II of Spain: "If there was any vice from which he was exempt it is only because nature does not permit perfection, even in evil."

Sadam Hussein added to the impression of his criminality when he gratuitously bombed Israeli civilian targets with Scud missiles, although Israel, acting in accord with the United States, had abstained from any military action of its own.

This was a deluxe war with heroes and villains sharply delineated and the justifications ideally defined. President Bush was elevated to heights of adulation in his own country—from which his precipitous decline became almost impossible to believe.

It was in this context that Bush enunciated the vision of a "new world order." He and other Western leaders clearly assumed that the Gulf War would become the paradigm governing future international relationships.

The center of this vision was the portrayal of the United Nations standing at the dawn of a new era in which it would resemble its original image as the powerful executant of a collective security system like that portrayed in the UN Charter itself.

The new order never came into existence. A readiness to defend the independence of oil-rich Kuwait did not entail any disposition to enforce international order among the successor states in Yugoslavia. For several months, the United States was humiliated by its own inaction and that of the major European powers in the face of horrifying tragedies in former Yugoslavia, where thousands of people, mostly civilians in Bosnia, were victims of brutal "ethnic cleansing" which evoked memories of the Holocaust.

The belief in a "new order" rested on the assumption that the Gulf War had established a precedent that would be emulated in other cases of aggression similar to the Iraqi assault on Kuwait. One of the illusions of the collective security principle is that all acts of unprovoked aggression are expected to meet with collective resistance in which the entire international community will be involved. It soon became evident that no major power would renounce its right of selective and discretionary response to conflicts, as and when they arose.

The touching hope that the world had discovered a guiding principle in harmony with the text of the UN Charter suffered one blow after another. In Somalia a humanitarian effort to save that country from famine whose torments were excruciatingly presented on television screens ended with the hasty withdrawal of U.S. and other forces from the beaches where they had landed in triumph some months before. The tyrannical junta that had dominated Haiti for several decades was able, with impunity, to chase a UN expedition back to the U.S. mainland. Huddled masses of refugees from Cuba, seeking asylum in Florida, were left to drown before reaching American territorial waters. Countless cease-fires in Bosnia, where French and British armies had been enlisted in UN peacekeeping forces, were concerted and violated in a single breath. The United Nations and its principal component powers looked on in agonizing impotence when hundreds of thousands perished in Rwanda at the hands of the Tutsi irregulars.

This is far from being the whole story of the 1990s. The Western victory in the Gulf has been succeeded by a cascade of events which heralded the triumph of democracy and market economies over the repressive Communist system. In Eastern Europe, South Africa, Ireland, and the Arab-Israeli area, leaders of nations and of repressed populations were willing to negotiate with those whom they would have puritanically rejected a few years before. It was the age of the "odd couples." Frederick de Klerk and Nelson Mandela, Yitzhak Rabin and Yasir Arafat, the prime ministers and nationalist leaders in Dublin and Belfast overcame traditional inhibitions and recognized negotiation as an unconditional duty, at least temporarily. Even the papal emissaries of the Vatican and delegates of Israel, the state of the Jews, celebrated ecumenical discourse as if the world of theology had turned a new corner. All of this had occurred after the encounters between American and Russian leaders at summit meetings had become routine. The idea of a new international concert in which a revived United Nations would preside over a serene world intersected bewilderingly with more familiar images of violence and affliction.

Illusion had flowed from a basic misunderstanding of the previous decades. The Western world regarded the Cold War as the single central source of international tension. The West had also exaggerated the degree to which the Soviet Union was responsible for instigating tensions. It underestimated deeper and more endemic conflicts which would be operative even if and when the Cold War came to an end. Nationalist rivalries, movements of religious fanaticism, unsolved territorial disputes, ancient prejudices and rancors, the sense of exclusion and discrimination afflicting underdeveloped countries which had thought that their political emancipation would be followed by a spectacular elevation in the conditions of their lives—all have been squeezed into a sort of Pandora's box. With the end of the Cold War, these tensions were set free from previous constraints. They could now breathe in their own right and seek their own horizons.

It is tempting but inaccurate to blame the UN for the world's remaining disappointments. The brain and heart of the UN are in the sole possession of its component parts. The power of correction lies in the capitals of the member states. Not much time had to elapse before it became evident that a decision to protect oil-rich Kuwait did not create any commitment to uphold the rights of oil-free Bosnia, or to bring sustained assistance to starving Somalia or Rwanda. All governments take their decisions individually in the name of national interest and then explain their decisions in terms of self-sacrificial altruism.

There is no doubt that the dream of a new international order focused largely on the United Nations. If there was to be a swift glow of hope it would surely send its radiance from New York's East River. The end of the Cold War seemed a golden opportunity for the UN to revive its original sense of promise. The fiftieth anniversary has now come and gone, leaving a stricken field and dying embers behind.

The United Nations was born more than half a century ago on such a high level of euphoria that a fall from grace was inevitable. Its founding conference at San Francisco in April 1945 resounded with slogans of redemption and hope. Many of those who attended the sessions may have felt that expectations were being set at an exaggerated level of optimism, but few would have predicted that, after fifty years, the peace organization would resemble the chorus in a Greek drama, expressing musical consternation at events which it has no power to control.

Disappointment would be less sharp if the UN founders had been content to claim that they were contributing an additional technique to the existing repertoire of diplomacy. But they were not in a mood to accept such a modest role. They were inspired by a utopian vision. "Inexorable tides of history," intoned one delegate, "are carrying us toward a golden age of freedom, justice, peace and social well-being." Another 1945 orator soared to biblical heights: "The UN Charter has grown from the prayers and prophecies of Isaiah and Micah."

Even statesmen renowned for their pragmatic temperament were caught up in this kind of intoxicating rhetoric. The U.S. secretary of state, Cordell Hull, was a Tennessean of austere moods who had never expressed an enthusiastic emotion in the past. He saw the establishment of the UN in 1945 as a messianic transformation: "There would no longer be any need for spheres of influence, for alliances, balances of power or any other of the special arrangements through which, in the unhappy past, the nations strove to safeguard their security or to promote their interests."[1]

This must surely rank as one of the most ill-considered statements in diplomatic history. International organization—which, after all, is a mechanism, not a policy or a principle—was here portrayed as a magic spell that would make all previous politics and diplomacy obsolete.

These salvationary hopes were based on the illusion that the American-Soviet-British alliance, which had won World War II, would command the future. This notion could have been refuted many months before by any serious historian.

American leaders had evidently convinced themselves that the UN, by its mere existence, would cause a new story, never heard or told before, to unfold across the human scene.

By contrast, the practitioners of traditional diplomacy have never spoken of themselves in the exalted tones used by the devotees of international organization. Professional diplomacy is dominated by a sense of limitation proceeding from a somber view of human nature. It pursues relatively modest goals, like prolonged stability, rather than a new era in the governance of mankind. It accepts the notion that conflict is endemic to human relations at all levels and that the most that can be done in the international field is to keep conflict within tolerable restraint. Diplomats, schooled in their own traditions, know that war prevented is a kind of peace, perhaps the only peace that many nations will ever know.

The movement for international organization was born in revolt against this unambitious view. Its devotees insisted on nothing less than "world peace under law." The theme was collective security. The central premise of this doctrine is that all nations have an equal interest in opposing specific acts of aggression and are willing to incur identical risks to resist them. This idea is so contrary to all of international experience that nothing short of charismatic authority could ever have brought it to birth.

Like all new religions, international organization did have a prophet who was deemed to speak consecrated words. President Woodrow Wilson was so assiduous in seeking European support for collective security that he failed to notice the lack of endorsement for it in his own American home.

Europeans who excitedly thronged the streets of Paris and London to greet Wilson in 1919 responded ecstatically to the tall, grave American who doffed his top hat in dignified salute. Presidents of the United States were an unknown species to them. No U.S. President had ever made such a pilgrimage before. Here was a man who represented the greatest power that had ever existed and had pledged himself to the most ambitious moral theory which any statesman had ever articulated. But the Europeans were not "sold" on Wilsonianism. They observed that principles of self-determination had not been extended in America to the yellow man or the black, or even to the southern states. They noted that the great American empire had been won by overpowering force. They thought it natural that Europeans would prefer the imprecisions of their own system to the vague idealism of a new system which Americans might fail to apply even to their own continent.[2]

As I have noted earlier, even the virtuous Wilson, after proclaiming his vision of "open covenants," went on to organize the most closed and conspiratorial peace conference in history. He closeted himself with the British, French, and Italian leaders—David Lloyd George, Georges Clemenceau, and Vittorio Emmanuele Orlando—and the "Big Four" drafted the treaty in a vengeful mood that seemed destined to prepare the ground for a new war.

Wilson died sadly amid the ruins of his own vision, but this did not deter the UN founders from seeking a second chance for collective security in the aftermath of World War II. The hope that the new international organization would have more success than its predecessor seemed well founded. For one thing, the UN was assured of universal membership. There were no signs of the American separatism which had spelled weakness for the League of Nations. Since American reservations had been regarded as the main cause of the league's failure, it was too innocently assumed that American participation would insure success. The fact that the three most powerful world leaders—Franklin D. Roosevelt, Joseph Stalin, and Winston Churchill—spent long hours at Yalta meticulously discussing the UN blueprint gave majestic strength to the internationalist cause.

The UN founders had an additional cause for optimism. The new peace organization, they said, would not be "toothless" like the League of Nations. It would be able to enforce its decisions. This idea came to expression in articles 43 and 47 of the UN Charter. A Military Staff Committee, composed of the five major powers (the United States, the Soviet Union, China, Britain, and France), would work out a plan for the mobilization of UN forces to be held ready under the command of the Security Council. For the first time in history collective security would be institutionalized. In 1945, high military officers from the armies of the five great powers gathered to discuss the idea of a UN military force.

The conventional wisdom in the West tells us that right-minded states wanted to create an enforcement mechanism but were frustrated by the persistent Soviet veto. The argument on these lines was developed at the height of the Cold War in the early 1950s. It is flagrantly untrue. As Secretary Hull told groups of senators, the veto provision was an absolute condition for American participation in the United Nations, and the small and medium-sized countries regarded the veto as a crucial defense against irresponsible majorities. A conscious decision was taken at San Francisco to avoid any attempt to subject the major powers to collective coercion. A representative of Sweden, in 1952, declared that the willingness of the small states to accept the obligations of the new security system was "dependent upon their assurance, derived from the veto provision, that there could be no United Nations call to action against a major power."[3]

It is too often forgotten that the UN Charter was written by men who had no knowledge of the existence of nuclear power. Those who knew this would surely not have advocated bringing American and Soviet forces into proximity in areas where their interests were discordant.

In 1947 the negotiations on article 47 inevitably collapsed. The five generals and eight admirals of the UN Military Staff Committee, brilliantly uniformed and bemedaled, would hold ritual meetings of a few minutes at the beginning of each month. The chairman would call them to order, announce that no speakers were inscribed, and propose the adjournment. A new chairman would take office for the next month by alphabetical rotation. A talent for perpetuating defunct institutions was to bedevil the repute of the United Nations in future decades. In this case, the monthly meetings were stopped before the farce became too patent.

This was a crucial development in world history. With the demise of articles 43 and 47, the UN had renounced the special quality that was meant to distinguish it from its predecessor. It had become like the League of Nations, an arena of debate with a capacity, still untested, to promote negotiated settlements, not by coercion but by consent. Collective security, as a formula for world order, was dead.

There was a brief period in which the United Nations appeared to be fulfilling a central role without the illusion of coercive force. In 1946 the Security Council ordained the withdrawal of Soviet troops from Iran and of French forces from Syria and Lebanon. In 1947 it played a major role in the decolonization of Indonesia. It resolved a potentially explosive dispute over Bahrain. In 1948–1949, after some failures, it instituted a durable cease-fire followed by a prolonged armistice between Israel and its Arab neighbors. Meanwhile, the General Assembly in 1947 had adopted a decision for the partition of Palestine which has been fiercely debated ever since, but which cannot be denied its character as a strong, daring act free from the defects of obscurity and procrastination which public opinion usually ascribes to international organization.

The disposition of the former Italian colonies (Eritrea, Somalia, and Libya) was also decided by votes in the General Assembly in 1949. More important, the Universal Declaration of Human Rights adopted at the end of 1948 may not have had direct influence on the behavior of states, but it is a bold and proud document, illuminated by a bright vision of humanity in its more compassionate and rational mood.

Strangely, Israel turned out to be the nation most beneficially affected by a UN action during this time, although few Israelis and Jewish leaders acknowledge this today. The Jewish people presented itself to the world community in the aftermath of World War II at the lowest ebb of its fortunes. Six million of its people, including a million children, had been slaughtered in Europe. The fame and dignity of the Jewish people had been dragged down in a whole decade of Nazi calumny. The promised homeland in Palestine was assailed by regional violence and international alienation. The victors of the anti-Hitler war showed no tendency to recognize the Palestinian Jews as a nation with political rights. At the constitutive conference of the United Nations, the Jewish leaders were humiliatingly seated in a distant balcony, looking down at the fifty nations, each sitting proudly behind its name and flag. A minority of them had any record of suffering and sacrifice in the unfinished war.

In swift succession, the UN responded to the horrors of the war by dramatically endorsing the Jewish claim to statehood in a partitioned Palestine. A year and a half later the UN revolutionized the juridical status of the Jewish people by the admission of Israel to membership in the United Nations. The admission resolution (273) led to Israel's full integration into the emerging international order, symbolized by membership in the functional agencies.

The subsequent spate of anti-Israeli assaults in General Assembly resolutions had fewer durable effects than did the UN's initial stimulus to the consolidation of Israel's juridical and international status. No historian has ever produced a scenario in which Israel's sovereignty could have been recognized so quickly in a world that lacked an international organization to fill the vacuum left by the end of British power. Later, the UN rejected five resolutions calling on Israel to withdraw from occupied territories without a peace agreement and, in a unique display of contrition, it annulled the 1975 resolution condemning Zionism as "racism."

But if the years 1945 to 1950 were the UN's half-decade of innovation, they still conveyed a premonition of marginality. All the major powers, including the United States, were determined to ensure that their own vital interests would not be submitted to UN jurisdiction. The Marshall Plan and the establishment of the NATO alliance were carried through in total disregard of the existence of the United Nations. In Europe, the Common Market and the other institutions of the European Community were born without any relationship to the United Nations. The Security Council, with great pomp and circumstance, established the Atomic Commission and the Commission for Conventional Armaments, but by 1949 both bodies had become inactive. It was evident that if Washington and Moscow ever intended to discuss arms control seriously, they would seek each other out in the privacy of traditional diplomacy. In the Korean War of 1950, the Security Council could pretend to be the commander of the UN forces under American leadership, but this fiction was only sustained by the fact that the USSR was obtusely absent from its seat and therefore from its veto-wielding capacity in the Security Council. In any case, President Truman preceded his recourse to the United Nations by a typical, unilateral decision to send forces first and explain their dispatch afterwards.[4]

It is very unlikely that collective security will ever regain preeminence as a central aim of international politics. Its reputation was based on six assumptions, none of which is valid in any contemporary context.

The first assumption is that states will identify their own security with the existing world order to such an extent that they will be prepared to defend that order by involvement in situations remote from their particular national interests.

The second assumption is that states will be able and willing to agree on the determination of aggression.

The third assumption is that the aggressor will be so weak or lonely that it will be possible to confront it with an international force superior to its own.

The fourth assumption is that states, inspired by the objective principles of collective security, will be willing to punish their closest allies as severely as they would proceed against their distant adversaries. Alliance, affinity, and common culture will simply melt away.

The fifth assumption is that states will renounce their power of separate decision about the disposition of their armed forces in areas in which their national interests are not involved.

The sixth assumption is that public debate in a permanent international conference will prove to be a more effective technique for reaching accords than the traditional method of compact, discreet negotiation.

None of these six assumptions is even remotely correct. Still less do all of them together constitute a realistic model for international behavior.

First, the loyalties built around the state are not transferrable to any notion of "world community."

Second, there is more obscurity than clarity in the definition of aggression. What is "aggression" for one is "self-defense" for another, and "national liberation" for a third.

Third, many small and medium-sized countries such as Egypt, Israel, Syria, Iraq, Iran, Turkey, and Ukraine now have the sort of fire power which an international force would find it hard to overcome. Even the Bosnian Serbs with their antiquated weaponry were able to intimidate UN peacekeepers and NATO air forces.

Fourth, nations, like human beings, are not immune from the laws of human nature; they do not react with equal and objective rigor, or indulgence, toward allies and adversaries alike.

Fifth, statesmen will not surrender their discretionary response on such crucial issues as the use of their own armed forces. Even the relatively innocuous use of forces for agreed peacekeeping and humanitarian purposes arouses strong resentments when casualties are incurred.

Sixth, a half century of experience has proved that traditional diplomacy, with its compact procedures and the occasional availability of reticence and secrecy, offers better chances of reaching accords than does a UN committed to public debate with massive participation.

My conclusion is that collective security failed to take root as the central principle of international life not because its opponents were of small mind or ignoble disposition, but more simply because it did not reflect the spirit of the age. It came on the scene in a world of nation states and called upon states suddenly to behave in a way in which states had never behaved in the whole of human history.

Once it was clear that the UN lacked enforcement powers, it should logically have deliberated about its future course. No such consideration occurred. It is still not clear what the United Nations wishes to be: an instrument for solving conflicts or an arena for waging them. The choice lies between the parliamentary and the diplomatic principle. The diplomatic principle tells me that I need my adversary's agreement. The parliamentary principle tells me that I don't need his agreement, since I can defeat and humiliate him by a majority vote. The two techniques require totally different psychological and procedural conditions. The unhappy choice of the parliamentary principle insured that the General Assembly would have a virulently polemical character.

The Wilsonian tradition praised collective security for its emphasis on publicity and its rejection of secrecy. But these are not aids to agreement. They are prescriptions for deadlock. As I argued in Chapter 4, without phases of secrecy and avoidance of publicity, agreements are virtually impossible. The role of secrecy in negotiation is not a mere relic of tradition. It is crucial. If a nation hears of a concession offered by its own representatives without also hearing of the corresponding concession made by the other party, indignation will erupt at the wrong time, with explosive results. A wiser Woodrow Wilson would have opted for "open covenants secretly arrived at," as Prime Minister Lester Pearson of Canada later suggested.[5]

One of the main weaknesses of the UN is its predilection for public debate in vast audiences with massive participation. Wilson eulogized the idea that "the great things remaining to be done can only be done with the whole world as a stage and in cooperation with the universal interests of mankind." Like many Wilsonian utterances, these words are a victory of eloquence over logic. The "whole world" is not really the most effective arbiter of disputes. There is more to be said for the negotiation of con-flicts between concerned parties whose destinies will be harmed by failure and served by success. As things stand, nations in the UN with no crucial interests in a dispute may band together to outvote states whose very survival is at stake.

With the Cold War ended, the world now seems to lack a strong incentive to reform its institutions. There has been no use of nuclear arms since World War II, the major powers have avoided confrontation, and some regional disputes have been solved. The international system, controlled by the power bal-ance and negotiation, has not been ideal, but it has not been so intolerable as to encourage UN members to seek new systems and procedures. The prediction that the choice for mankind would be between international organization and world war has been discredited. Prudent diplomacy in the traditional mold is a serious alternative.

Frustrated by the failure to construct a universal security sys-tem, international activists have sought compensations in other fields. One of the consolation prizes was alleged to be a repute for strong resonance. The UN can no longer sustain the claim of being the world's most powerful microphone. Report of debates is rare and scanty, and few news media maintain the bulky UN bureaus they had in the past. The addresses of foreign ministers in General Assembly debates pass from the orators' lips to obliv-ion without so much as a temporary resting place in the *New York Times*.

The relatively meager results for conciliation under UN aus-pices must be considered against the more impressive achieve-ments of conventional diplomacy. The years since the end of World War II have been a fruitful period for international con-ciliation, and most of the successes have been scored outside the UN. The Austrian State Treaty; the termination of the Ber-lin blockades; the Treaty of Rome establishing the European

Union; the end of the Algerian war; the American opening to China; the conclusion of the SALT I agreement; the Panama Canal settlement; the Ostpolitik agreements orchestrated by Chancellor Willy Brandt of West Germany, leading to the recognition of the existing European frontiers; the Rhodesia/Zimbabwe settlement; the European Security Conference at Helsinki; the Egyptian-Israeli peace treaty; the Israeli-Jordanian peace treaty; the Israeli-PLO Declaration of Principles; the dialogue between the United Kingdom and Ireland; the Israeli-Vatican reconciliation; the new agreements between the republics of the former Soviet Union and the Western states—all these together make an imposing list. They offer empirical evidence for a judgment that the public multilateral approach has been much less effective in conflict resolution than traditional negotiating techniques.

It was at least feasible to imagine that the UN might transcend the eclipse of collective security by emphasizing its "peacekeeping" role. This dimension of the UN was born during the crisis over the Suez Canal and Sinai in 1956–1957. Dag Hammarskjöld, Ralph Bunche, and Lester Pearson won merited honor for establishing the United Nations Emergency Force in Gaza and the Straits of Tiran. This measure, subsequently repeated in dozens of other areas of tension, had stabilizing effects. Dozens of volunteer soldiers sacrificed their lives nobly under the UN flag. But honesty compels the statement that peacekeeping is so remote from peacemaking or peace enforcement that it conveys the impression of "a poor man's UN."

Peacekeeping signifies the use of forces to monitor the maintenance of peace between states that have already decided to maintain peace. This does not have a heroic sound, but a real florescence of the peacemaking dimension would still give the UN an injection of prestige. In 1992, the UN Secretary General proposed an "agenda for peace" calling for a rapid reaction force composed of units stationed on home ground but ready to work together. This was ignored. There was no assurance that such units would ever be activated if the crux should come.

Unfortunately, the numerous successes of peacekeeping operations are shrouded in anonymity, while the failures shout from the housetops. Since the end of the Cold War there have been useful peacekeeping missions in Namibia, El Salvador, Cambodia, Mozambique, and Haiti, but these have been overshadowed by the dramatic fiasco in former Yugoslavia, where the United Kingdom and France formed the bulk of the forty-thousand-strong peacekeeping operation. These troops, despite their proud military lineage, were mocked, harassed, and humiliated by Serb warlords who competed in such actions as blocking the arrival of UN convoys and imposing starvation, as well as cruelly bombarding Muslim Bosnian populations. The modest aim of the peacekeepers was to insure that food and medical aid reached the populations of Sarajevo and other urban centers, but this could not be achieved without the UN occasionally fighting its way into its destinations and sometimes calling on NATO for air strikes against Serbian artillery.

In June 1995 a NATO air strike, strongly encouraged by the United States, provoked the taking of hundreds of British, French, and Canadian hostages by the Serbian authorities. The UN was placed in the position of passive attendance at its own humiliation. None of the deference once shown by governments and armies to the UN flag was practiced in Bosnia. The United States was shamed by advocating military measures on the part of its European allies without itself being exposed to risk, since it is an American axiom that American lives must not be risked in non-American contexts.

In the end, war-weariness prevailed. A breakthrough was achieved in 1995 when accords were signed at Dayton, Ohio, by the presidents of Bosnia, Croatia, and Serbia after prolonged negotiation under the auspices of the U.S. deputy secretary of state, Richard Holbrooke. This became possible when President Bill Clinton declared his readiness to commit twenty thousand American personnel to replace the UN peacekeeping force in former Yugoslavia. But sending lightly armed peacekeepers to areas where there is no peace to keep has brought international discredit to the UN system. Subsequently sending heavily armed NATO combat forces to keep a peace has compounded the confusion. It is a potentially fragile arrangement. It is generally believed that if there are serious outbreaks of violence with casualties among the U.S. peacekeeping contingents in Bosnia, there will be an outcry in Washington, together with pressure for the recall or withdrawal of the American troops.

If there is no hope for a real collective security system, and if traditional diplomacy is more effective than public rhetoric, what is there left for the UN to do? It is easier to diagnose the world's problems than to find a solution, and easier to formulate solutions than to get the public to accept them.

I believe that the UN would elicit a positive response if it devoted more attention to issues whose solution is beyond the capacity of individual states.

The inhabitants of the Earth now number 5.3 billion and at the present rate of increase will number 7 billion by the end of the twentieth century. More than half the world's present population suffer from varying degrees of malnutrition. The expectation of life, which exceeds seventy years in developed countries, is as low as thirty in parts of Asia and Africa. Hundreds of millions of people suffer from water-borne diseases for which remedies exist. Some 800 million adults throughout the world are illiterate. The most advanced countries are astronomically more prosperous than the least advanced. Science, technology, and industrial progress are still largely confined to the advanced countries which contain less than a quarter of the human race.

Planetary issues may now be the arena most congenial to dis-

cussion in multilateral agencies. When disasters occurred in Somalia and Rwanda, it would have been logical for the UN Secre-
tariat to be visibly leading the humanitarian effort. Yet the UN,
as reflected in the media, seemed to be marginal even in these
concerns.

Frustrated in its quest for a decisive role in international security, the UN can be credited with one momentous triumph for
its tenacious labors. It has given stalwart and audacious support to
the pageant of decolonization that has swept scores of new states
into the world community. Nothing does more to excite the
pride of new nations than the sight of their flags and names
around UN tables. It is impossible to narrate the story of the
South African transformation without tribute to the United Nations role.

The United Nations must face the fact that the multiplicity of
states in a world where sovereignty has lost a large part of its
meaning is the central political anomaly of our age. Social history
describes the expansion of a sense of community, from family to
tribe, from tribe to village, from village to city, from city to
nation-state. At every stage people have sought larger arenas in
which to express a sense of solidarity and cohesion. For some
reason the expansion of community seems to have got stuck at
the nation-state level. But the idea of a world community of
independent states is alive in the human imagination, though not
yet in the world of action.

Together with the multiplication of the nation-state as the
most important actor in today's international system there goes a
tendency to transcend nationhood through larger units of cooperation. Regional and multilateral bodies are proliferating. The
European Union seems to be an argument against premature
despair about the prospect of rising above nationalism into wider
groupings. Here we have fifteen sovereign states which have decided both to respect sovereignty and to transcend it. They have
diluted their sovereignty to some extent by accepting community

obligations. The fact that the federal implications of the European Union aroused serious reservations, first in France and later, with greater acerbity, in Britain, proves that a measure of erosion has already taken place in the once sacred idea of sovereignty. Unfortunately, however, it is difficult to draw any generalized conclusions from this relatively inspiring success. The European example is instructive without being infectious. It has little to convey to other regions.

The modern European Union is not a response to any compulsive historic necessity. Nobody can say that it was born because there was no alternative to its birth. By the time negotiations for the Treaty of Rome began in 1957, European recovery was already making excellent progress within national frameworks. There was also increased accessibility across boundaries and a disposition to renounce protectionist trade boundaries in the hope of stimulating the growth of expanding European markets.

The community idea in Europe took concrete form largely because of imaginative leadership. Konrad Adenauer, Robert Schuman, Alcide De Gasperi, Paul Henri Spaak, and Jean Monnet were gripped by an intense vision and were in a position to carry it to fulfillment. When Charles de Gaulle diagnosed the European determination to seek integrative relationships, he withdrew his nationalist objections and settled for a commanding French role in the community structures. The aged Winston Churchill belied his stereotyped image as an inveterate nationalist by spreading the European idea across Europe and the world with thunderous eloquence.

When I met Robert Schuman for the only time in the United Nations, I congratulated him on his perspicacity in concentrating on coal and steel, instead of proposing more provocative political integrationism. He replied that no normal human being is really interested in coal and steel, but it was necessary to make an innocuous beginning in order to achieve greater gains later on. In Jean Monnet's words: "This proposal has an essential political objective: to make a breach in the ramparts of national sovereignty which will be narrow enough to secure consent, but deep enough to open the way towards the unity that is essential to peace."[6]

In that spirit I was the first to propose a European solution for the structural interrelationship between Israel, Jordan, and the Palestinian state that will probably arise out of the current Middle East peace process. I alluded to the fact that European integration had begun with the Benelux Union in which three small states— Belgium, the Netherlands, and Luxembourg—established what became a prescription for the Six, then the Nine, then the Twelve, and later the Fifteen. This analogy for Israel, Jordan, and a Palestine state has been shamelessly plagiarized, but I do not repent of it. The idea is that three countries that do not seriously aspire to dominate each other should form a "community" in which sovereignty is balanced by community obligations.

The European Union is a success story, but it arose from exceptional circumstances. Until the late eighteenth and the early nineteenth century, leadership in Europe was in the hands of men who thought of themselves as Europeans first and members of nations second. Gibbon could speak of Europe as the Great Republic. So could Voltaire and Burke. The European leaders of the first generation were Christians and most of them Catholic. They listened to the same music, attended similar schools, and were driven by the same impulses. Yet the idea of a European Monetary Union, let alone an avowedly political integration, is already encountering difficulties. There does not seem to be a drive to common markets in regions outside Europe, even those which share common languages, as in Latin America. Nationalism is still alive and dominant.

There is little hope of a revival for international institutions without a strong impulse from an outside source of power. In the present world condition this can only come from the United States. But precisely at a moment in which the United States has total command of the UN system, it appears to be turning its back on the multilateral idea. The U.S. Congress is cutting support for UN peacekeeping and placing rigorous restraints on the use of U.S. forces for international service. The Clinton administration, which came to power amid strong expressions of support for multilateral frameworks, has accepted limitations beyond anything that previous administrations were prepared to envisage. A strong and prestigious liberal voice has reminded us that the "United States stands 20th on the list of nations making troop contributions to UN operations, well behind such world-powers as Bangladesh, Ghana and Nepal." In monetary terms, the United States "has cut back its allocation to a mere 0.15 percent of its domestic product, placing it last among the 21 industrial nations."[7]

The illogical alienation of the U.S. Congress from its previous devotion to world community is by far the heaviest factor working against the hope of a revived United Nations. The fact that the United States claims the full exercise of membership while refusing to pay its dues shows how far our world is from the visions that brought Roosevelt, Churchill, and Stalin together at Yalta in early 1945.

The UN had the misfortune of being born with a grossly inflated vision of its interventionist power. It must now moderate its ambitions. It is more affected by the circumstances of modern international relations than influential in changing those circumstances. All it can do is to create and maintain a mechanism to be put at the disposal of states which may use it for whatever they wish to achieve. But if we are talking about a mechanism rather than about a force that puts a mechanism to work, it is surely worthwhile to perfect its working and to sharpen its efficiency.

If expectations about the UN are reduced, it is still possible to reach a positive balance. It would be ridiculous if the first era of planetary interdependence were to find the world without a unitary framework of international relations. With all its imperfections, the UN system is still the main incarnation of the global spirit. It alone seeks to present a vision of mankind in its organic unity. There was never a time in human history when so many people crossed their own frontiers and came into contact with people of other faiths and nationalities. Parochialism is becoming steadily eroded by the new accessibility.

In the light of these slow but deep currents of human evolution, the idea of an international organization playing an assertive role in the pacification of our turbulent world may have to bide its time, but it will never disappear from view.

History and the future are firmly on its side.

9 The Oslo Negotiations

No expert on international affairs will ever need to apologize for failing to predict that a sensational breakthrough to peace in the Middle East would originate in Norway. Conventional wisdom had told us that the United States, as the only superpower, would be an indispensable partner of any negotiation between Israelis and Palestinians.

This belief was sustained by experience. The United States orchestrated the end of the Suez-Sinai war. It brought such intense pressure to bear upon Britain and France that these once proud imperial powers had no recourse except to abandon their ill-starred invasions of Egypt without securing any compensatory advantage for themselves. They had fought to secure the international character of the Suez Canal, but they withdrew from the battlefield in abject and catastrophic defeat.

Later, in concert with the United Kingdom, the United States helped to formulate UN Security Council Resolution 242, which has already become the documentary basis for a peace treaty with Egypt, a peace treaty with Jordan, and a negotiation with Syria. The United States has consistently supported the principle of "territories for peace." There has never been and probably never will be any other basis for a serious Israeli-Palestinian negotiation.

The idea that Norwegian, not American, statesmen were initiating a successful reconciliation between the Israeli and Palestinian peoples had bombshell effects in the diplomatic community and the media.

What came to be known as the "Norway Channel" originated during the 1992 Israeli elections when a Norwegian social scientist, Teje Larsen, met Yossi Beilin, a protégé of Israeli foreign minister Shimon Peres. Beilin was serving in the Knesset as an Opposition deputy awaiting a parliamentary election that would be charged with destiny for Israel and the Middle East. But there was no hint of future drama when the modest encounter between Larsen and Beilin took place early in 1993.

Larsen has none of the rigor and coldness that is often attributed to Scandinavian bureaucrats. He is a man of charm and vitality who has the ability to dominate a room by his presence. When Larsen and Beilin met each other in June 1992, the Middle Eastern dialogue was in sultry suspense. The Madrid Conference had come and gone, leaving no audible echoes. This was not surprising, since the Israeli prime minister, Yitzhak Shamir, was having a passionate love affair with the status quo. His ambition was to perpetuate the subjection of the nearly two million Palestinians, while filling the West Bank and Gaza with new Jewish settlements and closing off every prospect of Palestinian independence. Mr. Shamir is an engaging personality and it is he who described his policy (in an interview in the French daily *Le Monde*) exactly as I have portrayed it above, without any attempt at cosmetic concealment.

Beilin and Larsen were on the opposite side of the barricades. They had a relentless aversion to the condition of Gaza, where Palestinians eked out a somber and sterile destiny in the impoverished streets of a city which could compete with Haiti and

Rwanda as home to the most afflicted segment of the human race. Gaza was a land without a single smiling face, combining a fearsomely depressed economic condition with an explosive potential of violent revolt against what was, by any account, a harsh colonialist suppression. Gaza carried no message of hope or pride to Israel, which had ruled it for twenty-five years as an occupying power.

Gaza excited compassion in Larsen as a humane observer of misery and it spelled humiliation for Beilin as an Israeli, born on his own soil, and shamed by the filth and cowed servility of the Gaza streets. Gaza, apart from its other unsavory and malodorous attributes, was a demographic time bomb. Within a single generation, its population would expand twofold.

The overt task of Larsen and Beilin was to carry out a research project for a Norwegian study group called by the Norwegian acronym FAFO. This was a convenient device for evading the Israeli ban on a free flow of ideas between Israeli and Palestinian leaders. It should have seemed obvious that a Jewish people which had suffered more than any other nation from the ostracism and insult inflicted upon it by others would have been the last to embrace a principle of boycott in its own relations with its neighbors. But no paradox was too far-fetched to describe the vagaries of the Israeli-Palestinian relationship. In any case, Beilin and Larsen had their eyes fixed on horizons much broader than the mere vindication of the principle of encounter. They were seeking an Israeli-Palestinian reconciliation.

Both Larsen and Beilin were men of initiative who believed with a certain naiveté in the inherent solubility of problems. This had once been a typically Zionist concept, until the intoxication of the 1967 military victory diverted Israelis from their pioneering virtues.

But Israel was not the only actor in the Middle Eastern drama whose native astuteness was inhibited by theological fallacies. Contact with the PLO was forbidden by Israeli law—and, more absurdly, by the law of the United States. Back in 1973 the United States had been cajoled by Israeli leaders into the notion that formulations of Israeli and American policies had to be carbon copies of each other. The United States, like Israel, had adopted legislation which forbade negotiation with the PLO, with the result that American statesmanship could not maneuver in the area between Israeli, Palestinian, and U.S. positions. The diplomacies of the two nations were held in a Houdini-like knot. Unlike the legendary Houdini, however, they knew how to tie themselves up but had lost or forgotten the formula for successful escape. U.S. hostility toward the PLO virtually disqualified it from a mediatory function, and the Norwegians were providentially available to fill the vacuum.

The first task of Larsen and Beilin was to enlarge their range of Palestinian contacts without offending against Israeli law. Beilin suggested introducing Larsen to Yair Hirshfeld, who taught Middle Eastern economics at Haifa University. Larsen, Beilin, and Hirshfeld then sought encounter with Faisal Husseini, who resided in East Jerusalem. Husseini occupied a twilight status: he was not a PLO activist in any official sense, but he was known to be obedient to the PLO cause and a devotee of its ambition. The air of Israel was alive with electoral tension, and the prospect of a Labor victory bringing Yitzhak Rabin and Shimon Peres to power was serious enough to engage the media pundits. When Larsen, Beilin, Hirshfeld, and Husseini conferred in the tranquil corridors of the American Colony Hotel, a bulwark of Arab national sentiment, they were laying foundations for an Israeli recourse to originality and innovation. All this, however, depended on an Israeli electoral victory.

Opposition is a dreary fate in Israeli politics. When you are in the government you ask, "What shall I *do* today?" In opposition you can only ask, "What shall I *say* today?" Walter Bagehot, the British economist who wrote the standard book on the English constitution more than a century ago, described the cabinet system as the only regime in which the opposition is just as much a part of the system as is the government.[1] But Beilin, Larsen, Hirshfeld, and Husseini were after a more ambitious future than could be achieved by mere talk. They hoped to transcend the smallness of their country by mediating a solution of a major international crisis. This hope came close to fulfillment in June 1992, when the Norwegian-Israeli group had a taste of proximity to real power.

Their next contact was crucial. It led through the Norwegian government, where the foreign minister, Thorval Stoltenberg, had once inspired a failed attempt to bring Israelis and Palestinians together. Stoltenberg's ambition as a mediator had been shared by his deputy, Jan Egeland, who had written a dissertation for his doctorate on the subject of Norway's role in international mediation. Egeland was thirty-seven years old and believed that small states were not condemned to be no more than the satellites of major powers.

A major turning point for the Israeli-Norwegian group came when it enlisted Abu Alaa, who was a potential finance minister of a PLO administration. Abu Alaa's conviction was that a Palestinian-Israeli accord was more likely to spring from economic cooperation than from any political "happening." When Hirshfeld traveled to London to meet Abu Alaa, the Norway Channel had begun to lose its amateur status; it was entering the big leagues. With a prestigious Palestinian in close contact with the group, all that was now lacking was an official Israeli component.

Israeli politics was also liberating itself from self-imposed chains. When Secretary of State George Shultz announced in December 1988 that the United States, impressed by new tendencies of moderation and pragmatism in the Palestinian leadership, had decided to engage the PLO in active discussions, Shimon Peres criticized that sensible decision, declaring that "this was a sad day for Israel." It was a rare lapse from sanity for Peres. He should have said that this was a liberating day for Israel. The four years that remained before the Labor party would itself recognize Yasir Arafat as its partner were to become a diplomatic wasteland, empty of achievement and fertile with lost opportunities.

The breakthrough came when Rabin and Peres, responding to Abu Alaa's unwearying pressure, gave in on a matter that transcended protocolar niceties. Arafat was watching the talks from afar. He was insistent on knowing whether Rabin did or did not stand behind the discussions which had raised the hopes of the other participants.

When Rabin, after a show of reluctance, agreed that Uri Savir, the director general of the Foreign Ministry, would join the Norwegian and Palestinian "conspirators," the road was cleared. It was absurd to fear that an official of that rank, with a distinguished negotiating record, could attend a series of meetings without the approval of the Israeli prime minister. In a strikingly effective book on the Norwegian initiative, David Makovsky has written: "Upgrading the talks had significance beyond procedural wrangling and proved to be a pivotal turning-point. It was vital for Abu Alaa to believe that Rabin was identified with the Oslo talks. It transformed the Oslo track from academic, exploratory discussions to genuine, official negotiations. To Abu Alaa, it was an unmistakable sign that Rabin and not just Peres stood behind the Oslo Channel."[2]

The election of June 22, 1992, led to the first substantive change in Israeli policy and orientation in many years. It opened vistas of peace that the Israeli nation had never seen before. To the credit of Rabin and Peres, they declined to follow the illusion of "continuity" and opted for a sharp break with recent history. The willingness to engage Norwegian representatives in a mediation process proved that the new Israeli leadership was serious in its resolve to effect spectacular changes in national policy. It had made a clear determination to disengage Israel from the West Bank and Gaza and to seek partnership with Arafat.

The Norway Channel can only be understood in the light of developments in American policy during the early 1990s. The embarrassing truth is that American policymakers have always had a "hang-up" about official diplomatic recognition. It took them seventeen years, from 1917 to 1934, to recognize the Soviet Union. Seven years had to pass between 1965, when American leaders frankly admitted that they ought to recognize the Republic of China, and their actual award of that recognition in 1972. They had created a dilemma: first they persuaded their own public opinion to hate China, and then they underestimated their own capacity to implement a change of course.

In these and other cases the United States had confused diplomatic relations with morality and good will. Neither of these two components really belong to the diplomatic context. There is more sound sense in the observation of Winston Churchill: "The reason for having diplomatic relations is not to confer a compliment, but to secure a convenience."

Ignoring this advice, the United States had reached the end of the 1980s with a firm resolve to avoid regarding the PLO as a negotiating partner, when in reality PLO leaders were the only people worth talking to at all. In that obduracy the American leaders were blindly following Israeli vetoes. The lack of relations between the United States and the PLO prevented an American role in the Oslo talks and created the vacuum which Norway gallantly and creatively filled.

It has been the habit of ruling nations to seek negotiation only with compliant or "moderate" adversaries. The British, the French, and the South African governments avoided dialogue with the Indian Congress party, the Algerian FLN, and the African National Congress, respectively, until the lack of alternatives compelled them to change attitudes. Men and nations sometimes act wisely once they have exhausted all other options. In the end the rulers of nations have preferred to pursue contact with radical adversaries who could carry their constituencies rather than "moderate" representatives who could not.

The end of 1992 witnessed turning points in Norway. In January 1993 the strangely composed Norwegian-Israeli group met for the first time at the Borregård paper company in Sarpsborg, eighty miles from Oslo. The encounter was portrayed as an academic exercise. Hirshfeld had taken his friend Ron Pundak with him. The other participants were Teje Larsen; his talented wife, Mona Juul; the Norwegian foreign minister's wife, Marianne Heiberg, who was an authentic participant in the FAFO study; Abu Alaa, who alone gave an air of official weight to the proceedings; the deputy foreign minister, Jan Egeland; and Hanan Asfur, a PLO leader with links to Chairman Arafat himself and to Abu Mazen, the chairman's deputy. Asfur was to become a handicap to the gathering, since he had a deep dislike of fish, which would be the staple diet of the group. No Norwegian is ever disdainful of the culinary art.

The background of the January meeting and of the dozens that would follow in 1993 in front of log fires in comfortable Norwegian houses, with historic echoes of the Vikings, was, of course, the recent electoral victory that had projected Rabin and Peres into international prominence. Yet this reality nearly heralded the dissolution of the Norwegian initiative, since it sharpened Abu Alaa's consciousness of his own seniority and his consequent reluctance to be part of a relatively juvenile group. He constantly gave the other participants heavy hints: "I, after all, am a minister" was his slogan. He began an attritional campaign to upgrade the group, whose preponderance of "muddle-headed professors" worried him on all accounts. (Hirshfeld, a rotund Falstaffian figure, and Pundak, a leaner man, figured in Norwegian conversation as Laurel and Hardy.) The assiduous Norwegians and their Israeli guests spent dozens of hours formulating a declaration of principles that they hoped would win fame at the coming September assembly on the White House lawn.

The role of Norway has been unfairly overshadowed by a successful U.S. attempt to highlight American mediation as the decisive element in the Oslo accords. The truth is that the Oslo process was utterly Scandinavian. The Swedish foreign minister, Sven Anderson, had secured conciliatory exchanges between the PLO and a group of American Jews. But when the Swedish Socialists were defeated by a conservative government in 1991, Anderson believed that the Norwegian Socialists would have a better chance than Swedish conservatives to win the confidence of Prime Minister Rabin and Chairman Arafat. The final judgment must be that when the Norwegian group took command of the mediation, they handled it with supreme skill and tact.

There was a proud moment for the harassed Peres on August 27, 1993, when he flew with Norwegian foreign minister Jorgen Holst to a naval air base in California, where Secretary of State Warren Christopher and Dennis Ross were vacationing. The two visiting foreign ministers had the distinction of informing the U.S. secretary of state of a major milestone in international conciliation which had been largely pursued behind the back of the United States. Christopher is a statesman of integrity and he had no hesitation in congratulating the Israeli and Norwegian ministers on the success of their efforts. When I asked Peres how he knew that Christopher supported the Oslo initiative, he replied: "He smiled twice very briefly and said, 'You people have done a great job.'"

The Norwegians were the ideal mediators. They were free from pretentious attributes and defined themselves as bent on "facilitating" dialogue, not on mediating in any decisive sense. Like Dag Hammarskjöld in former days, they did not pretend to know the answers to the questions they posed. They preferred to work behind the scenes.

The peace process went on to celebrate its highest peak of success on the lawn of the White House on September 13, 1993. Three thousand dignitaries representing every sector of American national leadership gave resonant ovations to Prime Minister Rabin, Foreign Minister Peres, and Chairman Arafat—all of them crowned with Nobel laurels—while President Clinton praised each of the three for courage and devotion to Middle Eastern peace. The President himself received a well-merited boost in prestige for his part in the Middle Eastern grand design, over which he presided with eloquence and grace.

Rabin and Arafat had to overcome their deeply rooted distrust of each other in order to join the celebratory mood. When Rabin hesitantly shook hands with Arafat, a spontaneous roar of relief and joy went up from the crowd. The atmosphere seemed to presage an irreversible victory for the principle of reconciliation as a world view, with strong repercussions across all the remaining conflicts which afflicted the human race in the most violent of all the centuries. This might have been an exaggerated judgment of what, after all, was an achievement in a relatively parochial geographical context, but the sense of bells ringing across the world was felt by many nations in the aftermath of September 13, 1993. Nobody who participated in the jubilation that day will ever lose the memory from his heart.

For most of the next three years an optimistic appraisal of the peace prospect seemed to command the arena. But there were undercurrents of protest. A wave of terrorist assaults by suicide bombers who exploded themselves and dozens of Israeli civilians in buses overshadowed the peace process. There was a parallel outbreak of indignation from Israeli rightists and Jews of extremist temperament who preferred the illusion of "secure" boundaries to the newly available opportunities of a peaceful region.

There was none of the solidarity that had traditionally enabled Israelis to unite against common dangers. It was difficult to guess whence the most outrageous act of violence would come. It came first from a Jewish doctor of strongly orthodox faith who murdered twenty-nine Arab Muslims as they prostrated themselves in prayer. This obscene slaughterer of innocents was hailed by reverent supporters who eulogized his deed. The Likud leaders contravened a longstanding tradition of national unity in hours of peril by focusing a virulent campaign of assault on Prime Minister Rabin, whom the Opposition leader, Binyamin Netanyahu, described as "personally responsible" for the assaults of Palestinian extremists. Many Israelis saw a link of consequence between the frenzied tone of Opposition attacks and the horror of November 4, 1995, when a young man reared in a religious university planned and carried out an attack on the prime minister, murdering him by shots at the closest possible range and shattering his spine.

Rabin, the hero of Israeli wars, died within a few minutes of the assault, plunging the nation into a paroxysm of grief and shame that remains unassuaged to this day.

No citizen of Israel and no Jew in the world can justly acquit the opponents of the peace process of a measure of guilt for the extremist incitement with which they sped Rabin toward his doom. Netanyahu himself marched in processions which flaunted Rabin's name as a "traitor," sometimes garbed in an Arafat gallabiya, and once, probably without Netanyahu's knowledge, in a Nazi uniform.

And yet the peace process moved forward in its appointed sequence. Six of the country's main West Bank cities—Nablus, Jenin, Tulkarm, Ramallah, Bethlehem, and Jericho—celebrated the withdrawal of Israeli troops, who left no benign memories behind. A peace treaty with Jordan was signed amid rapturous applause in the U.S. House of Representatives, where Rabin and King Hussein embraced each other with authentic fervor. They really liked each other. I had represented Israel in several secret negotiations with King Hussein of Jordan after the Six-Day War of 1967. It was evident that he and I shared the intuition that our two countries held a common vision of the region in which our destinies were enacted. Proximity and a mutual entanglement of interests made a mockery of the hostility to which we each gave expression in several illogical wars. Israel and Jordan were in constant dialogue about our common concerns for regional security. Once peace between Israel and Jordan prevailed over artificial enmities, our two countries were able to hold impressive ceremonies in Washington and Cairo where we kept the peace process in well-focused view. After the murder of Rabin, Shimon Peres, who could easily have become an additional victim of the assassination, conducted the business of the Israeli nation with an authoritative and experienced hand.

Wisdom is born only when illusions die. There could never have been any progress toward a peace settlement in the Middle East until Arabs and Israelis liberated themselves from two delusions. There was the delusion of the Arabs that they could get their lost territories back without making peace with Israel. And there was a parallel Israeli delusion, shared by significant sectors of Israeli opinion, that Israel could get peace, or at least security, while retaining its rule over most of the territories occupied in the Six-Day War.

Each of these delusions was staggeringly unrealistic. Either one of them would have been sufficient to prevent a settlement; together they made progress to peace impossible.

By the 1990s, no serious Israeli believed any longer that Israel could get peace without reaching accords with the Palestinians on boundaries and security arrangements. And few if any Palestinians believed that they could regain the captured territories without making peace with Israel.

The peace process became possible because in the 1990s a whole cascade of attitudinal changes swept across the international scene. Some of these changes were generated by the end of the Cold War. If the nuclear giants were prepared to moderate their virulence and to seek accommodations, it would have been bizarre if there were no contagious fall-out across the world arena. Other changes came because an exhausted Middle East began to seek new perceptions of itself, with nations seeing their neighbors in a new and more humane light. The Palestinians grasped the fact that Israel's reactions were intrinsically defensive, even if they took aggressive form. Israelis knew that their Palestinian neighbors were not inherently different from other movements that include revolutionary violence in their list of bellicose methods, while themselves preferring what they call "international pressure."

Whatever the final outcome of the peace process, it has already transformed the Middle East. Nothing will ever be the same, as if the Oslo agreements had never been conceived, ratified, and concluded. No one on either side of the barricades has ever suggested that the Oslo agreements be superseded or annulled.

10 The Unfinished Quest for Peace in the Middle East

The appearance of a peace option in the Arab–Israeli conflict was not an isolated episode in world politics. It coincided with a broader movement toward international conciliation.

The major innovation, of course, was the spectacular end of the Cold War. It would have been little short of bizarre if such a momentous event had passed over the international system without leaving a strong impression across the entire arena of international relations. The winding down of the Cold War had already illustrated a perceptible war-weariness in international life. The U.S.-Soviet confrontation had ended in virtual deadlock; war was evidently not a viable solution of anything, and no alternative set of relationships had taken its place.

Diplomacy, so often accused of traditionalism, had suddenly been ventilated by fresh winds. This was the age of "odd couples." Leaders of nations were holding civilized discourse with adversaries whom they would have puritanically shunned a few years ago.

This tendency produced a thaw in some of the most obdurate international conflicts. Behind twin microphones stood F. W. de

Klerk and Nelson Mandela, speeding apartheid in South Africa toward its overdue demise. Hardly had we rubbed our eyes at this spectacle when Yitzhak Rabin and Yasir Arafat took their places in a similar ritual, closely followed by King Hussein and Prime Minister Rabin, opening horizons toward a new Middle East. Next, the Vatican—author of the medieval expulsions, the Inquisition, and the humiliating ghetto system—sent its representatives to Jerusalem to mark its reconciliation with Israel, the state of the Jews. A long saga of Jewish suffering and gentile intolerance came to an official end.

Next came the prime ministers of the United Kingdom and Ireland, outlawing the bomb and gun, and virtually legitimizing the Irish Republican Army as a negotiating partner. All this only a few years after George Bush and Bill Clinton began to regard Mikhail Gorbachev and Boris Yeltsin as partners in a journey toward international peace.

Even the leaders of Serbia, Bosnia, and Croatia signed an accord under U.S. pressure in Dayton, Ohio, in November 1995, with the aim of stabilizing the cease-fire in former Yugoslavia.

This never became the only norm of international conduct, and I am aware of contrary examples which are still taking a tragic toll. But the strange encounters that I have evoked are more than individual episodes. Diplomatic discourse was liberating itself from entrenched routines. World opinion no longer tolerated the idea that rulers have the right to appoint their own representatives—and also those of their adversaries. The ANC, the PLO, and the IRA all had abrasive chapters in their résumés, but so did their more powerful interlocutors. Rabin, Peres, and Arafat deserved their celebrations, but if the Israeli leaders had accepted dialogue with the PLO a few years earlier, many lives might have been saved. The same was true of those who spurned negotiation with the ANC in South Africa and with the IRA in Ireland during the wilderness years.

Together with this change in the principle of discourse, we

witnessed a new approach to agendas. Negotiators used to fill their rhetoric with arguments about the origins of conflicts and the culpability for their eruption. In the new diplomacy, the question "Who provoked and who responded?" was marginalized. The issue now was how to quench the fires, not how to hold interminable debate about who kindled them. Pragmatic compromises usurped the place hitherto occupied by reciprocal exchanges of self-righteousness.

Even the United Nations experienced a new spasm of lucidity. International agencies had previously allowed the issues of origins and culpability to monopolize their agendas and to exhaust the disputants. The United Nations joined, and may even claim to have inspired, the impulse and movement of the modern diplomatic age. The UN General Assembly went so far as to express contrition for its previous anti-Zionist frenzy. Its adoption of a joint Israeli-PLO resolution legitimizing the Middle Eastern peace process would have been inconceivable two or three years before.

Diplomacy can only gain in public esteem by shaking off the intrinsically insoluble arguments about virtue and conscience and concentrating on more practical goals. Reciprocal self-interest is the central theme.

Another illusion that now suffered eclipse was one that used to tell us that it was possible for one nation to rule over a foreign population without consent. A central law of the new diplomatic age is that coercive jurisdictions have disqualified themselves through experience and suffering. Some form of coexistence must take the place of military occupations. We Israelis are not colonial newcomers to the Middle East. Israel's roots in the region are older and deeper than the roots of any other people on any other soil. But Israel is undoubtedly alien to the Palestinian people over whom it has been exercising absolute rule for more than twenty-five years. What the British could not do any longer in India or the French in Algeria or the Dutch in Indonesia or the

Belgians in Congo and Rwanda or the Soviet Union in Afghanistan or the United States in Vietnam, and what the white Afri-
cans could no longer do in South Africa, despite their overwhelming power, never became possible for Israel.

The map of Israel extending its jurisdiction from Golan to
Suez, with nearly two million Arabs under its rule, became an
international absurdity. It is not in the nature of a modern democracy to rule over two million members of a different nation
without offering them either equal justice as citizens or a chance
to establish their separate jurisdiction.

The initial debate about the future of Arabs and Jews in their
common land was concerned with the principle of partition. The
basic document about the future of our area was lucidly formulated in 1947 by the UN General Assembly and its committees.
"The political unity of the Palestine area can only be maintained
at the cost of rigorous repression." The international judgment
said simply that neither of the two nations could justly maintain
its rule over the other, irrespective of whether it was the Palestinians, who then claimed the right to rule over the Jewish minority,
or an Israeli state, which found itself ruling over a large Palestinian Arab population for more than a quarter of a century.

Ours is a land of two nations, two faiths, two tongues, two
national sentiments, two historic experiences. Duality is written
so deeply on the history and geography of this country that any
subjection of one nation to the other would be morally fragile
and inherently explosive. This means that sovereignty and territory have to be shared by both peoples and not monopolized by
either. It was on the wings of the historic partition decision, in
which the United States and the Soviet Union joined together,
that Israel was able to put its flag into the winds of history.

Israel was most vulnerable when it ruled the entire area between
the Suez Canal and the Golan Heights. The map showing the full
extent of that jurisdiction had a solid and reassuring look. In

reality, we were greatly overextended. We were governing areas that had previously been parts of three other states. We could only continue to hold them by maintaining great armies in areas hundreds of miles apart from each other, and we were doing this without regional or international consent.

I reiterate my conviction that the Six-Day War during which Israel rose up against deadly peril was a war of salvation. I take nothing back of what I then said in describing our danger. I used the following words: "As righteous as the defense of freedom at Valley Forge, as just as the expulsion of Hitler's bombers from British skies, as noble as the protection of Stalingrad against the Nazi hordes, so was the defense of Israel's security and existence against those who sought our nation's destruction. Never have freedom, honor, justice, national interest, and international morality been so righteously protected."

But to say this is not to say that the same justice and logic would apply to the continued maintenance into the third decade of the military administration established in 1967.

Israel's new leaders were not the first to understand the inadmissibility of that condition. The decisive turning point came in 1979. Prime Minister Menachem Begin decided that Israel should renounce all its assets and establishments in Sinai, and also make provision for the withdrawal of the Israeli civil and military administrations in the West Bank and Gaza, in order to make way for "self-government" under which "the inhabitants of the West Bank and Gaza should govern themselves."

It would be ridiculous to look back, with any sense of consolation, to the map that showed Israel ruling the whole area between Golan and Suez from 1967 to 1973. Those years were feasible only amid a bloodbath. Twenty-five hundred Israeli dead to protect Israel's positions in Sinai in 1973. More than six hundred Israelis lost in the effort to maintain Israeli positions along the canal against artillery bombardment. And more than five hundred Israeli soldiers lost in Lebanon, including Beirut, in a war that was supposed to put an end to the action of radical Palestinian nationalists. One of the conditions that encouraged the peace process was Israeli disillusion with the experience of annexation and domination.

The Gulf War of 1990 was not an Israeli enterprise; we were urgently persuaded by the United States, as the leader of the victorious coalition, to adopt a policy of conspicuous unobtrusiveness. This is not a characteristic Israeli posture. But most Israelis understood that a military campaign that would blunt the force of Iraqi aggression for at least several years would be a more tangible gain for Israel than anything that could be achieved by action to disrupt the anti-Iraqi coalition.

The decline and fall of the Soviet Communist empire had prodigious effects on Israel. Together with the opening of the gates for Jewish emigration to Israel came a vast change in Israel's security. Suddenly, the whole weight and bulk of the former Soviet Union and the Eastern European countries were transferred from the negative to the positive scale of Israel's strategic balance. Without Soviet support of Arab hostility during the Cold War, Soviet arms supplies, and the closing of Israeli access to international agencies, Israel would never have faced existential dangers.

The conversion of Russia to the support of the peace process inaugurated by the United States was a transforming event. Israelis were astounded as their flag went up in Moscow, Warsaw, Prague, and Kiev, as well as in vaguely remembered capitals of Slovenia, Croatia, Bosnia, Khazakhstan, Uzbekistan, and even Armenia.

Syria never thought of attacking Israel, except on three conditions that no longer exist. The first condition was that Egypt would be attacking Israel from the south. The second condition that made Syria so intransigent was the fact that it had a Soviet safety net. Syria knew that if it got itself into trouble on the battlefield against Israel, which it often did, it could rely on the intimidation and pressure of the Soviet Union to halt any Israeli advance. Syria could, therefore, fight its wars with limited liability. Its attractive alternatives were to win or not to lose.

The third condition for Syrian military activism was that there would be a friendly and fraternal Iraq at Syria's side. But Syria and Iraq fought on opposite sides in the Gulf War. Syria has not yet agreed to make peace with Israel, but it certainly can be relied upon to avoid war. In the Middle East we should be thankful for small mercies and should therefore cease to call them small.

It may be true, as some American observers have said, that Syria wants peace with America more than it wants peace with Israel. There is nothing incongruous in that idea. What is certain is that Syria would not find anything like peace or stability if, after its alienation from the Soviet Union, it were to suffer a crisis in its relations with the United States.

The PLO was not destroyed in the fighting in Lebanon, as some Israelis like Ariel Sharon hoped. It showed a phoenix-like capacity of regeneration. Arafat and his assistants were the weakest of the Arab nations in every material calculation of power, but they represented the principle of legitimacy.

When Egypt, the ostensible center of Arab power and culture, signed a peace treaty with Israel in 1979, not a single other Arab state followed Cairo's brave example. Yet when Arafat and Rabin shook hands on the White House lawn fourteen years later, the entire Arab world with its twenty-two capitals began a wild rush to endorse the Palestinian decision. Syria announced a "strategic decision" for peace with Israel, Jordan concluded a peace treaty, and Morocco, Tunisia, Oman, Qattar, and Mauritania invited Israeli participation in economic conferences at Casablanca, Amman, and Cairo.

Only Binyamin Netanyahu, the newly elected Israeli leader, failed to comprehend the centrality of the Palestine issue in the Middle East. He wavered for months before making his first awkward contact with the Palestinian leader, whom he continued to treat with a lordly condescension and disdain.

A remarkably perceptive American scholar has written: "States do not simply pursue power; they pursue a variety of ends that are dictated by concepts of legitimacy. Such concepts act as powerful constraints on the pursuit of power for its own sake, and those states which disregard considerations of legitimacy do so at their own peril. Legitimacy constituted, in Vaclav Havel's phrase, 'the power of the powerless.' Realists who look only at capabilities and not intentions are at a loss when intentions change so rapidly."[1]

Since the overriding Arab belief holds the Palestine issue as the criterion of legitimacy, it was obtuse of Israeli leaders to seek avenues of achievement in other fields.

The crowning accomplishment of Israel in the framework of the peace process was to have established a contractual relationship with the mainstream Palestinian organization. To endanger this in favor of a few scattered settlements in the heart of Arab population centers was to take a broad step in a march of folly.

Arafat's followers are now doing more than almost anyone else to combat the dissident terrorists of Hamas and Hizbollah.

It remains painfully true that not even the powerful Israeli army, with its renowned intelligence services, has ever been able to insure total security against individual Palestinian terrorists. Even in areas under exclusive Israeli control, the plague of the suicide bombers has not been deterred. It is true that when Israelis and Palestinians meet, they have divergent versions of their previous histories. In a sense, this liberates diplomats for the task of negotiation and leaves space for academic historians to tell us what went wrong in the past.

The Palestinians are the central figures in the Middle Eastern peace process. As Israel's closest neighbors, they continue to come and go between Israel and the Arab world, bringing important skills into the region's expanding markets. As a Nobel laureate together with former Prime Ministers Rabin and Peres, Chairman Arafat is a pivotal figure in the region. His relations with Israel are controversial but, in central issues, cooperative.

The Arab country most likely to play a creative role in Middle East development plans is the Hashemite Kingdom of Jordan. King Hussein has never pretended that he represents the leadership of the Arab world. It is, however, undeniable that cooperative projects are more feasible in the Israeli-Jordanian relationship than in any other.

This arises from the proximity and reciprocal accessibility of the two countries, and from the intimate links that have united them in the past.

Is it not absurd that there should be two separate ports: one at Eilat and one at Aqaba, only a few kilometers apart? Should there not be joint authorities enabling both countries to exploit their access to East Africa and to the prosperous economies of the Pacific Rim? Is it really an enactment of history that the Dead Sea should always be dead, with Jordan and Israel each capable of preventing its neighbor from utilizing what is still one of the great concentrations of pharmaceutical raw materials? Might there not be a real exuberance of fruitful contacts if those searching for the roots of Western civilization could pass from the Israeli capital in Jerusalem across the river to Petra, seat of the old Nabatean civilization, and thence southward to witness the glories of Egypt's pharaonic legacy?

Something of this new accessibility is already active among Israel, Jordan, and Egypt. Jordan, with its stable institutions and cordial relations with all the other Arab states, is the least affected of all by the turbulence that sometimes erupts across the Middle East.

King Hussein, as the senior statesman in the region, is the stalwart rock of the Middle East's ambition to communicate examples of stability and creative energy across the region and beyond.

An Israeli leadership that cannot live harmoniously with King Hussein will never live harmoniously anywhere in its own region.

It is impossible to strike a balance in appraising the peace process without reference to the general expansion of Israel's international network of interests. Strategic predominance, together with the peace process, enabled Israel to achieve dazzling diplomatic successes. Israel now has diplomatic relations not with a mere 50 but with 160 countries. These include the giants of the Third World—India and China—along with Malaysia, Indonesia, Tanzania, and others still to come. Israel's flag has flown in Cairo, Oman, Tunisia, and Morocco. There are fruitful and promising contacts with many countries in the Gulf area. Even Saudi Arabia endorsed the Oslo peace process and virtually eliminated the main pressures of the Arab boycott against Israel. Instead of being the most isolated country in the world, Israel could become the least isolated.

When the first Israeli president, the illustrious Chaim Weizmann, ascended to his high office, he received a communication from an Asian government that wished to honor the Israeli president with a gift. This was to be an Indian elephant of vast bulk and weight. President Weizmann asked me, his very young and junior associate, to draft a courteous letter saying that, in his native village in Russia, there used to be a proverb among the Jewish farmers: "Never accept a present that eats."

I do not say that the success of the peace process will lead to utopia. I do, however, declare that the failure of the peace process would lead to an inferno of explosive antagonisms and volcanic hatreds. Generations might have to pass before anybody would attempt such a peace project again. Many currents of policy and interest had to converge in order to bring the peace process to birth. If it were to end in failure, peace itself and the very hope of it would probably be eclipsed.

Yitzhak Rabin and Shimon Peres were the first Israeli leaders to give priority in Israel's foreign policy to relations with the Arab and Muslim worlds. To say this is not to downplay previous explorations, but it was not even physically possible to shake hands with those who confronted us with clenched fists. There are no precedents for a nation to negotiate successfully with those who deny its identity and sovereignty.

It was not until December 7, 1988, that the Palestinian leaders recognized Israel's right to exist in peace and security as a neighbor in the Middle East. When Norwegian statesmen persuaded Yasir Arafat to embody this attitude in a declaration of principles, truly a window of opportunity was opened.

Until that date Israel had always had to seek its allies at great distance from its own region. In World War I, the auspices were provided by Britain. In 1947–1949 the United Nations, in a rare burst of American-Soviet cooperation, gave powerful support to Israel's statehood. For "a brief shining moment" in the mid-sixties, France supplied an embattled Israel with aircraft and a crucial strategic deterrent. For some decades the United States has created an Israeli military predominance which contrasts sharply with Israel's previous vulnerability.

No country has been more in need of external aid than Israel— or more successful in obtaining it. During most of the past half-century the American-Israeli relationship assumed all the aspects of a strategic alliance.

A very important result of the peace process was the Israeli breakthrough to the Arab and Muslim worlds. At the time of Netanyahu's election on May 29, 1996, Israel had operative relations with Egypt and Jordan, contacts at various levels with Morocco, Tunisia, Mauritania, Oman, and Qattar, with a clear opening to other Arab states in North Africa and the Gulf, an enhanced relationship with Turkey, and—most significant of all—a closely negotiated agreement with the Palestine Authority.

There was a better environment in the United Nations and the Vatican than Israel had ever enjoyed since becoming a member of the United Nations in 1949. Conferences at Casablanca and Amman were auguries of new economic relations on a universal scale.

Every one of the countries that maintains any kind of positive relationship with Israel based its policies on the current peace process as expressed in the Oslo accords. Remove those documents from the repertoire of Israel's jurisprudence and Israel's new international position would be blown away like snowflakes before the wind.

There is now a serious danger that the network of agreements constructed by the previous government has begun to unravel. Egypt is contentious, Jordan is irritated, Morocco declines to receive Israeli leaders who had easy access in the Rabin-Peres era, Qattar and Oman have postponed the establishment of embassies, and the expected expansion of Israel's relations with Arab countries in North Africa and the Gulf has come to a halt.

These developments result from the tone of Israeli rhetoric and policies since Netanyahu's election. The challenge for the prime minister and his colleagues is to review the balance between their domestic pressures and their international interests, with the aim of giving the international factor greater weight than they initially did.

The expansion of pro-Israeli sentiment across the world was facilitated by international developments, many of which were unconnected with the parochial complexities of Middle Eastern politics.

Fundamentalist virulence has not been eliminated, but it now has to struggle hard against pragmatic and realistic tendencies that were invisible a few years ago. The idea that only Israel has moved while the Arab world has stood still does not deserve to be taken

seriously anywhere in the world. It resembles an alibi for diplomatic rigidity more than a lucid commentary on events and
movements.

It follows that if the gains of the peace process for Israel are
allowed to lose their effect, it may become impossible to bring
them to renewed existence ever again. In the vacuum thus created, the field will be open for radicalism, violence, and despair.
The eclipse of the peace process would inflict on Israel the most
serious debacle that it has ever known.

Rabin led the Israeli establishment into the bold understanding that no external friendships can fully compensate Israel for
the absence of a harmonious regional order. Israel's task today is
not only to proclaim its own rights but also to bring those rights
into accord with the rights and interests of others.

There is need for a period of historic reflection. We remember
that our land was twice ravaged and its people dispersed because
our forebears, with all the exaltation of their poetry and the depth
of their prophetic insights, never achieved interaction with neighbors who are far less predatory now than they once were. We
should be inspired by our history without being enslaved by it.

One thing is certain: Israel cannot live peacefully outside the international order that mocks the pretensions of unilateral power.

The Middle East peace process has lived through two sharply
divided moods and conditions. The first stage found the idea of a
peaceful region in the ascendant. Israel had developed relations at
various levels with fifteen Arab states and with most of the nations that were formerly republics of the Soviet Union. There
was a clear prospect of progress toward what would credibly have
become a "new Middle East."

The election of a new and less peace-oriented Israeli government in May 1996 arrested this momentum.

The first actions of the Netanyahu administration were promising. The newly elected leadership defied the narrowness of its

majority—less than a third of 1 percent—and adopted the Oslo accords as its central theme. After a six-month delay it allowed a new project for the division of Hebron to go forward. A small enclave of a few hundred Jewish settlers surrounded in Hebron by a massive population of 120,000 Arabs moved by extreme interpretations of Islamic faith does not sound like a prescription for domestic stability, but in previous ages Arab communities and Israel have often lived in conditions that defied logic. These situations have not always collapsed.

Unfortunately, the current relationship between Israelis and Arabs has been marked by an erosion of mutual trust. The two incidents that have shattered the trust do not ostensibly seem worthy of the consequences that have ensued. One was the opening of a tunnel in September 1996 close to the Dome of the Rock, where Jewish and Muslim religious interests converge. Under the Oslo accords, Israel agreed to the arming of the Palestinian police, which turned its arms against Israeli forces. Sixty Arabs and sixteen Israelis were killed during that nightmare confrontation.

Shortly thereafter, Jewish settlers began work on a new building project at Har Chomah. Arabs saw this as an attempt to fragment the areas of their own habitation with the aim of making Palestinian statehood unfeasible in the long term. The PLO used this admittedly wrong-headed Israeli action as a reason for freezing all cooperative security relationships between the two populations and their leaders.

Then came a terrifying raid in a Jerusalem market by two suicide bombers leaving dozens of dead and wounded. The Israeli government did not divulge any information, if it had any, about the possible identity or ideology of the perpetrators. The Israeli reaction consisted of draconian punishments inflicted on the entire populations of the West Bank and Gaza in a degree that the United States, the European Union, and other friends of Israel considered excessive. Funds meant for the Palestinian Authority were confiscated by Israel with doubtful legality. This occurred without any suggestion that the Palestinian Authority could have been guilty of the bombing outrage.

This time the tensions constituted a virtual sundering of common Israeli and Arab interests across entire populations. Egypt was disgruntled, Jordan irritated, the Tunisian and Moroccan diplomats were abandoning their posts, and the prospects of an economic reunion at Qattar in the Gulf were dubious. Little seemed left of the creative structures and contacts which the Rabin and Peres administrations created in the region.

Yet I continue to believe that the Middle East has been irreversibly transformed by the peace process. The parties have said things to each other that were never said before. Written commitments have been exchanged.

To this day no one in power on either side has rejected the Oslo accords. The opportunities for peace remain greater than they were before the memorable talks in Norway. There is hope that active mediation by U.S. secretary of state Madeleine Albright will restore something of the spirit and atmosphere that prevailed on the White House lawn in September 1993.

There are, however, no guarantees for the future. Dedicated opponents of peace can still dismantle the accords bit by bit until every element of friendship, trust, and cooperation has been undone.

For Palestinians the peace process represents a chance to take possession of their destiny and go forward in peace and hope. For Israel there is a chance of real security and an opportunity to assert its democratic and humane origins. No sane Arabs believe any longer that Israel, the most powerful regional nation, is destructible—least of all by the chronically weak Palestinian Authority.

For both peoples a path has been shown in which the opportunities transcend the dangers. It is a difficult path and daunting, but unless it is pursued, generations may pass before anyone will attempt such a peace process again.

Afterword

It is impossible to deny that the convergence of the Soviet utopia with the Nazi inferno in the late 1930s nearly caused the democracies to lose the war. If this had occurred, Churchill's prediction of a new "Dark Age" would not have seemed an exaggerated figure of speech. This was a crisis from which the world narrowly escaped. Then, in 1945, before the Western powers had gained the minimal time necessary for psychological adjustment, the prospect of a Soviet-American war loomed on the horizon.

The peril was averted by two courageous decisions. One of them was the American resolve to avoid the fatal error of the interwar period (1918–1939), when the United States had withdrawn behind a barrier of protective tariffs and isolationist legislation, leaving Europe to its catastrophic fate. This time, the United States rallied behind President Truman and his congressional allies to establish a robust and dynamic "containment" policy that contrasted sharply with the feeble appeasements of the 1930s.

The other decision was that of European statesmen, chastened by experience, to launch a cooperative economic and political order inspired by democratic principles and community structures. Leaders of the stature of Konrad Adenauer, Jean Monnet, Robert Schuman, Paul Henri Spaak, and Alcide de Gasperi— fortified reluctantly by de Gaulle and enthusiastically by Churchill—made European unity their watchword and guiding light. When a democratized Japan added its economic power to that alliance, the international balance was transformed in a manner that would have aroused the envy of prewar Europe.

An intellectual phalanx of great brilliance and versatility sustained the statesmen of the post-1945 era with their insights and eloquence.[1]

The ideology of the new era was expressed by my own Cambridge mentor, Herbert Butterfield: "The underlying aim is to clarify the principles of prudence and moral obligation which have held together the international society of states throughout its history, and still hold it together."

"Prudence and moral obligation" do not sound like passionate battle cries of the kind that inspire men and women to martyrdom, sacrifice, and heroic feats. The most that could be said of them, as Isaiah Berlin assiduously pointed out, was that they "might yet prevent mutual destruction and, in the end, preserve the world."[2]

Dean Acheson, whose role in the formulation of the Truman policy has been underestimated, was indeed a man of many certainties and few doubts. He gave the impression of aloofness, sharpened by conspicuous formality of dress and speech, but he had a developed sense of personality. His diplomacy was in the classical tradition; the emphasis was on European humanism, reticence, and pragmatism, based on common interests and free from sentimentality. His travels were almost exclusively conducted within the European orbit that would have been familiar to the participants of the Congress of Vienna.

The Truman-Acheson principles were serenely unaffected by the idiosyncrasies of their successors. They survived the embarrassing tendency of John Foster Dulles to ascribe his intensely pragmatic insights to divine guidance.

One writer has described the Eisenhower era as in fact an exercise in continuity: "He ended the Korean War, he refused to intervene militarily in Indochina, he refrained from involving the United States in the Suez crisis, he avoided war with China [over Quemoy and Matsu], he resisted the temptation to force a showdown after Berlin, he stopped exploding nuclear weapons in the atmosphere."[3]

Here again, "refused," "refrained," "resisted," and "stopped" are not heroic words. They do imply that a degree of abstentionism from folly is often an important dimension of wisdom, even if it is sometimes disparaged as "passivity."

The truth is that American policies showed more constancy than diversity until the unhappy adventurism in Vietnam and the astonishing resourcefulness of Henry Kissinger in the relationship that he and Nixon fashioned with Mao Tse-tung, Deng Xiao-ping, and Chou En-lai in China.

American policymakers have never been free from confusion about the central purpose of their dialogue with the outer world. They arduously strive to convince other nations of their moral rectitude, while the questions other nations ask about the United States concern American strength and resolve. Doubt about the degree of American readiness to defend its own interests is felt by friends and adversaries alike.

There was once an apprehension that the trauma of Vietnam may have generated an atmosphere of penitence going far beyond objective necessity and coming close to a flight from the very principle of power. It was understandable and correct for Americans to feel that their commitment in Southeast Asia was not viable or capable of success, and even that American interests were not crucially at issue. But there was no tendency for Americans to be similarly inhibited from defending their positions in Central Europe or asserting them in Russia, as well as in the NATO and Iraqi-Iranian contexts.

Henry Kissinger, who is still a media magnate, has been manifestly apathetic about the long-term future of the Third World, and his skepticism about America's ability to impose its own concepts of human rights on its friends, let alone its adversaries, is deeply rooted in his own intuition and experience. Nor has he ever embraced the myth that international organization can replace diplomacy and politics and thus illuminate a path to a messianic era of harmony and perfection. His reluctance to adopt these dogmas of conventional American sentiment has exposed him to the kind of criticism meted out to Galileo for declining to proclaim the flatness of the globe and its centrality within the solar system.

A U.S. administration in which opposing parties occupy the White House and the congressional leadership is more likely to adopt a reactive than a dynamic role in foreign affairs. The American system seems built more for checking than for balancing. It lacks the incentive for the forward thrust that carried the Roosevelt administration forward to international leadership and gave the Johnson administration the basis for far-reaching domestic reforms. This modest appraisal, however, may have to be revised if external crisis imposes itself on the American nation to a degree unpredictable at this time.

The United States has never found it easy to express the central reality of being unable either to escape from the world or to dominate it. An America in which utopia is simply not available may have to be content with small mercies, in which case it might be better not to keep calling them small.

I make no apology here for declining to follow convention in predicting a "Pacific Century." This expectation is based on the extraordinary success of four small entities—South Korea, Hong Kong, Taiwan, and Singapore—in rising to phenomenal levels of productivity. These NIE (New Industrial Economies) societies account for a great part of the wealth of Asia, but not of its population. If we are going to witness a Pacific Century, more emphasis will have to be put on Japan and China. But Japanese dynamism seems to be encountering a period of arrest, and China is separated from the rest of Asia by an abrasive record of human rights violation.

China and India have not yet succeeded in creating an intense educational vitality. The United States, Japan, and Western Europe spend 6 percent of their product on education, while India and China are satisfied with 3 percent. This does not signify that India and China are backward in education, but they are producing a glut of graduates beyond their employment capacities and are thus creating a movement of skilled manpower toward the developed world.

The question is whether developing countries can really create small enclaves of technical skills amid hundreds of millions of impoverished people. Another problem is the contradiction in developing countries between the emphasis on education and technology and the fact that there are still millions of peasants in these countries who have not yet emerged from the agricultural age.

Africa and Asia have had brilliant leaders who carried them from colonial subjection to independence with all its external glories, such as embassies and seats in international agencies. But these leaders were much more brilliant in achieving independence than in knowing what to do with it. The flags are not enough. Men and women awaken on the morrow of independence celebrations to find that they may be free in every constitutional sense and yet lose the essence of their freedom in the throes of illiteracy, starvation, rampant disease, and want. Sometimes these legacies of colonialism are even aggravated by the transition from tutelage to freedom. Many such leaders have attracted world attention by the pathos of their struggle for freedom. I recall my own meetings with Pandit Nehru, Jomo Kenyatta, Léopold Sédar Senghor, Norodom Sihanouk, Lee Kwan Yew, Sukarno, Sekou Toure, Félix Houphouët-Boigny, and Zulfikar Ali Bhutto, few of whom have shown the same consuming interest in the dull prose of economic planning as in the more facile satisfactions of international diplomacy.

Third World leaders would be on more solid ground in their discourse with the West if they would take their stand on mutual cooperation between the developed and developing worlds rather than on pretensions of moral superiority. The developing countries do not always offer other nations social visions worthy of emulation. Idi Amin in Uganda, "Emperor" Jean Bedel Bokassa in the Central African Republic, Pol Pot in Cambodia, and the new Chinese leaders are not exactly models of fidelity to the human rights conventions.

Even Japan appears to other continents as an asset and a problem. On the one hand, it combats the tendency to arrange the intercontinental relationship in conformity with an East-West syndrome. On the other hand, the United States would welcome a wider access to Japanese markets and a larger Japanese contribution to regional defense. In the latter context, however, the harsh memories of Japanese military conquests act as a brake. The difficulty the United States has in arguing too vehemently with Japan is aggravated by Japan's indispensability to any international system in which America has a central place.

Samuel P. Huntington's effort to categorize nations in terms of civilizations with which they are said to identify is gallant but unavailing.[4] It breaks down on the very issue of identity-consciousness that lies at the root of the effort. It is all very well to exhort peoples to define themselves as "Islamic-Confucian" or in terms of "the West versus the Rest" and to take consolation from such statements as "We have a Turkish nation feeling the same sentiments as the Azerbaijanis." But the truth is that a long time has always had to elapse before peoples change their habits of defining their own identity.

What we call the "developing world" still lacks coherence. The phrase itself tries to bridge a gulf between states like Niger, Mali, and Haiti, with average per capita annual incomes of $300, and states like South Korea, where the figure is $5,000, and Singapore, with its prodigious $9,070, and some Gulf states, where the statistics soar above recognizable horizons. There is not even a unified will. The world measures prosperity by economic progress, but some movements in India and in the Muslim world deny that economic progress is a valid ideal, insisting that salvation be sought in self-denial and spirituality. The Pacific Century is not with us yet.

We are left with the reality that the majority of mankind still define themselves in the old terms of nation-states. There is a paradox here. Never was the world more united in its destiny—and more fragmented in its structure. In theory, the individual nation-state should be in eclipse. It is not a viable unit of security. It does not function as an autonomous economic system. It cannot hope to solve environmental problems within its own limits. Yet there has never been such a proliferation of nation-states as in the last half century. The international system is decentralized through the existence of nearly two hundred units of alleged sovereign decision.

The multiplicity of nation-states in a world where sovereignty has lost a great part of its meaning is the central political anomaly of our age. The need for men and women to be identified with compact social groups seems to be as elemental as the need for food, shelter, and perpetuation of the species, and no community exerts a more potent hold than the nation-state as a focus of inspiration, solidarity, and sacrifice. Despite the parallel growth of regional and supranational institutions, there is no sign that the nation-state is being superseded as the main source of allegiance and social pride.

Those who predicted that the sense of nationhood would decline based their judgment on the inadequacy of nationhood as an expression of real independence. They gave too little weight to the fact that nationhood is largely a spiritual ideal and as such is immune to the erosion of its secular relevance. In the words of the French historian Joseph-Ernest Renan: "A nation is a soul, a spiritual principle. A common glory in the past, a common hope for the future. To have done great things together, to wish to do them again—these are the conditions for the existence of a nation."

Yet there is a paradox within the paradox. Together with the proliferation of nation-states is a growing tendency to transcend nationality through larger units of cooperation. Regional and multilateral bodies such as the European Union, the Organization of African States, the Arab League, the Muslim fundamentalist associations, the network of UN institutions, the Organization of Petroleum Exporting Countries, and multilateral agencies proliferate, while multinational corporations make national frontiers irrelevant as expressions of economic power. The interaction of governments is only one of the arenas in which nations encounter each other. Our world is fragmenting and integrating at the same time.

The most promising feature of post–Cold War diplomacy is its restrained mood. There is little self-delusion. Problems of war and international rivalry may never be "solved," but there is a prospect that the antagonisms may be kept in restraint. This may sound unattractively sober in comparison with the yearnings for world community that fill many of the noblest chapters of literature, but diplomats, scarred by experience, have no choice but to inhabit a middle emotional ground between excessive skepticism and exaggerated hope.

Notes

Chapter 1

1. See Henry Kissinger, *Diplomacy* (New York: Simon and Schuster, 1994), p. 799. This is Kissinger's summary of claims made in the *Time* article.
2. Charter of the United Nations, June 26, 1945, 1 U.N.T.S., preamble.
3. Robert E. Sherwood, *Roosevelt and Hopkins* (New York: Harper Brothers, 1950), p. 870.
4. *Foreign Relations of the United States. Diplomatic Papers: The Conferences at Malta and Yalta 1945* (Washington: Government Printing Office, 1955), p. 972.
5. Harry S. Truman, *Memoirs*, vol. 1: *Year of Decisions* (Garden City, N.Y.: Doubleday, 1955), p. 82.
6. Seweryn Bialer, "The Death of Soviet Communism," *Foreign Affairs* 70, no. 5 (1991): 181.
7. Winston Churchill, *His Complete Speeches*, vol. 6, ed. Robert Rhodes James (New York: Chelsea House, 1974), p. 6161.
8. Ibid., vol. 7, p. 7290.
9. George F. Kennan, *Memoirs, 1925–1950* (Boston: Little, Brown, 1967), p. 253.

Chapter 2

Epigraph: Arthur M. Schlesinger, Jr., *The Cycles of American History* (Boston: Houghton Mifflin, 1986), pp. 69–70.

1. Kenneth Thompson, "Ethics and International Relations: The Problem," in *Ethics and International Relations,* ed. Kenneth Thompson (New Brunswick, N.J.: Transaction Books, 1985), p. 17.

2. Thucydides, *The Peloponnesian War,* trans. Richard Crawley (New York: Modern Library, 1982), p. 351.

3. Harold Nicolson, *The Evolution of Diplomacy* (New York: Collier, 1966), pp. 23–24.

4. François de Callières, *On the Manner of Negotiating with Princes,* trans. A. F. White (Boston: Houghton Mifflin, 1919), p. 64.

5. Nicolson, *Evolution,* p. 19.

6. Niccolò Machiavelli, *The Prince and Discourses,* trans. Max Lerner (New York: Modern Library, 1940), p. 528.

7. Reinhold Niebuhr, *Moral Man and Immoral Society* (New York: Scribner's, 1932), p. 267. Niebuhr attributes these words to Hugh Cecil.

8. Henry Kissinger, *Diplomacy* (New York: Simon and Schuster, 1994), pp. 62–63.

9. Felix Gilbert, *To the Farewell Address: Ideas of Early American Foreign Policy* (Princeton: Princeton University Press, 1961), p. 45. See John Adams to Secretary Livingston, Feb. 5, 1783, in John Adams, *Works,* ed. Charles Francis Adams, vol. 8 (Boston, 1853), p. 35.

10. George Washington, "Farewell Address, 1796." See Gilbert, *To the Farewell Address,* p. 145.

11. Harold Nicolson, *Peacemaking 1919* (London: Constable, 1945), pp. 29–30.

12. Ibid., pp. 157–58.

13. Kissinger, *Diplomacy,* p. 30.

14. Ibid., p. 32.

15. Nicolson, *Peacemaking 1919,* p. 163.

16. Hans J. Morgenthau, *Politics Among Nations,* 5th ed. (New York: Alfred A. Knopf, 1973), pp. 397–401.

17. Willy Brandt, former chancellor of the Federal Republic of Germany, and Lester Pearson, former prime minister of Canada.

Chapter 3

1. George F. Kennan, *At a Century's Ending: Reflections, 1982–1995* (New York: W. W. Norton, 1996), p. 315.

2. See Anthony Eden, *Full Circle* (Boston: Houghton Mifflin, 1960), pp. 519–20.

3. Ibid., p. 108. Every statesman has seen clearly through the fallacies of other statesmen's analogies.

4. See George W. Ball, *The Past Has Another Pattern* (New York: W. W. Norton, 1982), chap. 7.

5. John F. Kennedy, "Inaugural Address," in *Let Us Begin: The First 100 Days of the Kennedy Administration*, commentary by Martin Agronsky et al. (New York: Simon and Schuster, 1961), p. 144.

6. Emphasis added. For an alternative translation, see Ibn Khaldun, *al-Muqaddimah: An Introduction to History*, trans. Franz Rosenthal (New York: Pantheon, 1958), vol. 3, pp. 308–10.

7. David C. Hendrickson, review of *Pay any Price: Lyndon Johnson and the Wars for Vietnam*, by Lloyd C. Gardner, *Foreign Affairs* 75, no. 2 (March/April 1996): 150.

8. Will and Ariel Durant, *The Age of Reason Begins* (New York: Simon and Schuster, 1961), p. 267.

Chapter 4

1. Charter of the United Nations, June 26, 1945, 1 U.N.T.S., art. 2(7).

2. Ibid., art. 1(3).

3. Arthur M. Schlesinger, Jr., *The Cycles of American History* (Boston: Houghton Mifflin, 1986), p. 99.

4. David Riesman, "The Danger of the Human Rights Campaign," in Fred Warner Neal, *Détente or Debacle* (New York: W. W. Norton, 1979), p. 56.

5. A. Doak Barnett et al., "Developing a Peaceful, Stable, and Cooperative Relationship with China," National Committee on American Foreign Policy Report (July 1996), pp. 25–26.

Chapter 5

1. Woodrow Wilson, *War and Peace: Presidential Messages, Addresses, and Public Papers (1917–1924)*, vol. 1 (New York: Harper and Brothers, 1927), p. 159.

2. Ibid., p. 192 (emphasis added).

3. This was also further evidence in support of Harold Nicolson's observation that "[Wilson] and his conscience were on terms of such incessant intimacy that any little disagreement between them could easily be arranged." See Harold Nicolson, *Peacemaking 1919* (London: Constable, 1945), p. 163.

4. Walter Lippmann, *The Public Philosophy* (Boston: Little Brown, 1955), p. 20.

5. Gordon A. Craig and Francis L. Loewenheim, eds., *The Diplomats, 1939–1979* (Princeton, N.J.: Princeton University Press, 1994), p. 680.

See James Reston, *The Artillery of the Press* (New York: Harper and Row, 1966), pp. 30–31.

Chapter 6

1. Winston Churchill, speech at Edinburgh, Feb. 14, 1950, in *His Complete Speeches,* vol. 8, ed. Robert Rhodes James (New York: Chelsea House, 1974), p. 7944.
2. Speech before the House of Commons, May 11, 1953 (emphasis added).
3. Henry Kissinger, *Diplomacy* (New York: Simon and Schuster, 1994), p. 507.
4. In modern times, heads of state are usually resentful of the climbing propensities of other heads of state. President Eisenhower and British Prime Minister Harold Macmillan were good friends, but they had nothing good to say about each other's summit meetings. Eisenhower winced at the spectacle of Macmillan brandishing his white fur hat in the streets of Moscow, and Macmillan made fun of Eisenhower's invitation to Khrushchev to tour America in an effort (as described by Macmillan) "to substitute jollification for discussion."
5. Harold Nicolson, *Peacemaking 1919* (London: Constable, 1945), pp. 171–72.
6. In 1960 the UN General Assembly was graced by an exceptional plurality of heads of state. The spectacle of these lordly personages having to take their turn at the cafeteria appealed to populist sentiment, but the leaders themselves were not gratified. They returned to their habit of ensuring that each one of them would be in the United States alone at a given time. When the confluence of their excellencies was repeated in 1995, each of them made his or her entries and exits in swift succession and none of them showed a consuming interest in listening to the others.
7. Gordon Craig, "The Professional Diplomat and His Problems, 1919–1939," *World Politics* 4, no. 2 (January 1952): 155–56.
8. George W. Ball, *The Past Has Another Pattern* (New York: W. W. Norton, 1982), p. 458.
9. Hedley Bull, *The Anarchical Society* (New York: Columbia University Press, 1977), pp. 178–79.
10. John Kenneth Galbraith, *A Life in Our Times* (Boston: Houghton Mifflin, 1981), p. 391.
11. Ibid., p. 392.

Chapter 7

1. This has led some scholars, such as Michael Walzer, to regret that no act of demonstrative warning was attempted in 1945. He has written: "In

the summer of 1945, the victorious Americans owed the Japanese people an experiment in negotiation." The only counterargument is that such an idea did not belong to the atmosphere of 1945. See Michael Walzer, *Just and Unjust Wars* (New York: Basic Books, 1977), p. 268.

2. Peter Rodman, "The Missiles of October: Twenty Years Later," *Commentary* 74, no. 4 (October 1982): 40.

3. Robert S. McNamara, *In Retrospect: The Tragedy and Lessons of Vietnam* (New York: Random House, 1995), p. 111.

4. Ibid., pp. 160–61.

5. Ibid., p. 275.

6. Winston Churchill, *His Complete Speeches,* vol. 7, ed. Robert Rhodes James (New York: Chelsea House, 1974), p. 7800.

7. The Catholic bishops in the United States tormented themselves and their constituencies for long, weary years. In 1982 the bishops' declaration emphasizing the need for complete immunity of civilian populations seemed to be a denunciation of nuclear deterrence. But Pope John Paul II at the United Nations declared that "in current conditions deterrence based on balance is morally a step on the way to progressive disarmament." Walzer admits the paradox: "We threaten evil in order not to do it, and the doing of it would be so terrible that the threat seems in comparison to be morally defensible." See Walzer, *Just and Unjust Wars,* p. 274.

8. Michael Klare, *Rogue States and Nuclear Outlaws: America's Search for a New Foreign Policy* (New York: Hill and Wang, 1995), pp. 132–33.

9. Michael Klare's study includes a reminder that "since 1990, the United States and Pakistan have repeatedly clashed over nuclear proliferation." See Klare, *Rogue States,* p. 157.

10. Richard N. Haass, *Intervention: The Use of Military Force in the Post Cold War World* (Washington D.C.: Carnegie Endowment for International Peace, 1994), p. 21.

11. Walzer, *Just and Unjust Wars,* p. 85.

12. Manfred Halpern, "The Morality and Politics of Intervention," in *Moral Dimensions of American Foreign Policy,* ed. Kenneth Thompson (New Brunswick, N.J.: Transaction Books, 1984), p. 85.

Chapter 8

1. Cordell Hull, *Memoirs,* vol. 2 (New York: Macmillan, 1948), p. 1648.

2. American leaders who had qualms about their own rectitude sometimes resolved them by appeal to divine judgment. When President William McKinley wished to annex the Philippines in 1897, he spent the whole night on his knees in prayer for celestial guidance. It is cer-

tain that he would not have accepted a negative answer. In the event, his supplications continued until the Heavenly Will was worn down by attrition. The United States made war against Spain and moved into the Philippines.

3. Inis L. Claude, Jr., *Power and International Relations* (New York: Random House, 1962), pp. 160–61. The Mexican delegate at San Francisco said, cogently, that under the UN Charter, "the mice could be stamped out, but . . . the lions would not be restrained." Ibid., p. 159.

4. International law does not always provide a solution. One of the most tormenting aspects of collective security is that decisions which are of immaculate legality become harmful if they are isolated from the chain of consequence. An example of this was the Anglo-French decision early in 1940 to resist the Soviet invasion of Finland. This action, including the expulsion of the Soviet Union from the League of Nations, was juridically correct in terms of the League Covenant. Finland was entitled to receive international aid against aggression. But Britain and France nearly found themselves at war with Hitler's Germany and the Soviet Union at the same time! Thus the Anglo-French action in Scandinavia, while exemplary in legal terms, would, if maintained, have prevented the eventual defeat of Hitler. It is possible to be legally correct and empirically reckless at one and the same time.

5. See Lester Pearson, *Diplomacy in a Nuclear Age* (Cambridge, Mass.: Harvard University Press, 1959), pp. 36 and 43–44.

6. Jean Monnet, *Memoirs,* trans. Richard Mayne (London: Collins, 1978), p. 296.

7. Arthur Schlesinger, Jr., "New Isolationists Weaken America," *New York Times,* 11 June 1995: 15E.

Chapter 9

1. Walter Bagehot, *The English Constitution* (1867; rpt. Ithaca, N.Y.: Cornell University Press, 1966), p. 72.

2. David Makovsky, *Making Peace with the PLO* (Boulder, Colo.: Westview Press, 1996), p. 45.

Chapter 10

1. Francis Fukuyama, *The End of History* (New York: Free Press, 1992), pp. 15–16.

Afterword

1. Few chapters of statesmanship have been enlivened by writers and thinkers as incisive and analytically perceptive as Reinhold Niebuhr,

Hans Morgenthau, George Kennan, Henry Kissinger, Raymond Aron, Herbert Butterfield, Walter Lippmann, Quincy Wright, Hersh Lauterpacht, Arnold Toynbee, Kenneth Thompson, Barbara Tuchman, Henry Steele Commager, Arthur Schlesinger, Jr., Michael Walzer, Michael Howard, Inis Claude, Jr., Connor Cruise O'Brien, Gordon Craig, and Stanley Hoffmann.

2. Isaiah Berlin, "The Decline of Utopian Ideas in the West," in *The Crooked Timber of Humanity: Chapters in the History of Ideas* (New York: Alfred A. Knopf, 1991), pp. 47–48.

3. Robert A. Divine, *Eisenhower and the Cold War* (Oxford: Oxford University Press, 1981), p. 154.

4. Samuel P. Huntington, *The Clash of Civilizations and the Remaking of the World Order* (New York: Simon and Schuster, 1996).

Index